Diabetic Diet After 60 for Beginners

Take care of your health with super easy and quick recipes and a 30-day meal plan for lasting diabetes control

Franz Geissler

© **Copyright 2024 by Franz Geissler - All rights reserved.**

This document is geared towards providing exact and reliable information in regard to the topic and issue covered.

- From a Declaration of Principles which was accepted and approved equally by a Committee of the American Bar Association and a Committee of Publishers and Associations.

In no way is it legal to reproduce, duplicate, or transmit any part of this document in either electronic means or in printed format. All rights reserved.

The information provided herein is stated to be truthful and consistent, in that any liability, in terms of inattention or otherwise, by any usage or abuse of any policies, processes, or directions contained within is the solitary and utter responsibility of the recipient reader. Under no circumstances will any legal responsibility or blame be held against the publisher for any reparation, damages, or monetary loss due to the information herein, either directly or indirectly.

Respective authors own all copyrights not held by the publisher.

The information herein is offered for informational purposes solely and is universal as so. The presentation of the information is without contract or any type of guarantee assurance.

The trademarks that are used are without any consent, and the publication of the trademark is without permission or backing by the trademark owner. All trademarks and brands within this book are for clarifying purposes only and are owned by the owners themselves, not affiliated with this document.

Access the bonus

Scroll to the end and scan the QR code

Take care of your health with super easy and quick recipes and a 30-day meal plan for lasting diabetes control 1
Franz Geissler 1
1. Understanding diabetes after 60 7
    1.1 The impact of aging on diabetes 10
    1.2 Dietary principles for managing diabetes 13
    1.3 Creating a daily meal structure 16
2. The essentials of a diabetic diet 18
    2.1 Understanding the glycemic index 20
    2.2 Reading and interpreting nutrition labels 22
    2.3 Creating balanced meals 25
3. Easy and nutritious breakfast recipes 27
    3.1 Almond and blueberry smoothie 27
    3.2 Spinach and feta omelette 28
    3.3 Cinnamon apple oatmeal 30
    3.4 Chia seed pudding with berries 31
    3.5 Avocado toast with poached egg 32
    3.6 Low-carb yogurt parfait 33
    3.7 Turkey and spinach breakfast burrito 34
    3.8 Cottage cheese and peach bowl 35
    3.9 Buckwheat pancakes 36
    3.10 Veggie-packed frittata 37
    3.11 Tofu scramble with kale 38
    3.12 Quinoa breakfast bowl 40
    3.13 Smoked salmon and cream cheese bagel 41
    3.14 Nutty banana bread 42
    3.15 Sautéed mushrooms and tomatoes on toast 43
    3.16 Protein-rich breakfast bars 44
    3.17 Green detox smoothie 45
    3.18 Ricotta and pear toast 46
    3.19 Southwestern tofu hash 47
    3.20 Pumpkin spice oatmeal 48
4. Wholesome lunch recipes for optimal health 49
    4.1 Turkey and spinach stuffed peppers 49
    4.2 Quinoa and black bean salad 51
    4.3 Broccoli and cheddar soup 52
    4.4 Grilled chicken caesar salad 53
    4.5 Vegetable stir-fry with tofu 54
    4.6 Mediterranean chickpea wrap 55
    4.7 Zucchini noodle caprese 56

- 4.8 Lentil soup with spinach 57
- 4.9 Avocado chicken salad 58
- 4.10 Baked salmon with dill yogurt sauce 59
- 4.11 Roasted vegetable quiche 60
- 4.12 Cucumber and hummus sandwiches 62
- 4.13 Spinach and feta stuffed chicken 63
- 4.14 Asian beef salad 64
- 4.15 Shrimp and avocado taco salad 65
- 4.16 Butternut squash and chickpea curry 66
- 4.17 Pear and walnut salad 68
- 4.18 Turkey meatball soup 69
- 4.19 Eggplant and mozzarella bake 70
- 4.20 Cold beet and yogurt soup 71

5. Satisfying dinner recipes 72
- 5.1 Grilled salmon with dill yogurt sauce 72
- 5.2 Chicken and vegetable stir-fry 73
- 5.3 Turkey and spinach stuffed peppers 74
- 5.4 Lentil soup with kale 74
- 5.5 Zucchini noodles with pesto 75
- 5.6 Baked tilapia with lemon and herbs 76
- 5.7 Vegetarian chili 77
- 5.8 Grilled chicken caesar salad 79
- 5.9 Beef and broccoli 80
- 5.10 Spaghetti squash with marinara sauce 81
- 5.11 Pork tenderloin with apple cider glaze 82
- 5.12 Shrimp and asparagus stir-fry 83
- 5.13 Eggplant parmesan 84
- 5.14 Cauliflower rice pilaf 86
- 5.15 Balsamic glazed salmon 87
- 5.16 Chickpea and spinach curry 88
- 5.17 Stuffed acorn squash 90
- 5.18 Quinoa and black bean stuffed peppers 92
- 5.19 Roasted chicken with root vegetables 94
- 5.20 Mediterranean vegetable stew 95

6. 30-day diabetic meal plan 96

1. Understanding diabetes after 60

Understanding diabetes after 60 is crucial for managing your health and well-being as you age. Diabetes is a chronic condition that affects how your body processes blood sugar (glucose), and it becomes increasingly important to manage it effectively as you grow older. This chapter will delve into the basics of diabetes, particularly focusing on its impact on individuals over 60, and will cover the physiological changes that occur with age and how they influence diabetes management. Additionally, it will highlight the importance of diet in maintaining healthy blood sugar levels and overall well-being.

As we age, our bodies undergo various physiological changes that can affect the way we manage diabetes. One of the most significant changes is the decrease in insulin sensitivity. Insulin is a hormone produced by the pancreas that helps regulate blood sugar levels. As we get older, our cells become less responsive to insulin, which can lead to higher blood sugar levels. This condition, known as insulin resistance, is a common precursor to type 2 diabetes. Furthermore, the pancreas may produce less insulin with age, making it even more challenging to keep blood sugar levels in check.

Another factor to consider is the decline in kidney function that often accompanies aging. The kidneys play a crucial role in filtering waste products from the blood, including excess glucose. When kidney function diminishes, it can lead to an accumulation of glucose in the bloodstream, exacerbating diabetes symptoms. Additionally, aging can bring about changes in body composition, such as an increase in body fat and a decrease in muscle mass. These changes can further contribute to insulin resistance and make it more difficult to manage diabetes effectively.

Cardiovascular health is another critical aspect to consider when managing diabetes after 60. Diabetes significantly increases the risk of heart disease and stroke, and this risk becomes even more pronounced with age. High blood sugar levels can damage blood vessels and nerves, leading to complications such as high blood pressure, atherosclerosis (hardening of the arteries), and peripheral artery disease. Therefore, it is essential to monitor and manage not only blood sugar levels but also blood pressure and cholesterol levels to reduce the risk of cardiovascular complications.

One of the most effective ways to manage diabetes and its associated risks is through a well-balanced diet. Diet plays a pivotal role in regulating blood sugar levels and maintaining overall health. For individuals over 60, it is particularly important to focus on nutrient-dense foods that provide essential vitamins, minerals, and fiber while helping to control blood sugar levels. A diet rich in whole grains, lean proteins, healthy fats, and plenty of fruits and vegetables can help stabilize blood sugar levels and support overall health.

Understanding the glycemic index (GI) of foods is also crucial for managing diabetes. The glycemic index measures how quickly a food raises blood sugar levels. Foods with a high GI cause rapid spikes in blood sugar, while those with a low GI result in a slower, more gradual increase. For individuals with diabetes, it is advisable to choose low-GI foods to help maintain stable blood sugar levels. Examples of low-GI foods include whole grains, legumes, non-starchy vegetables, and most fruits. On the other hand, high-GI foods such as white bread, sugary snacks, and processed foods should be limited.

In addition to choosing the right foods, portion control is essential for managing diabetes. Overeating, even healthy foods, can lead to weight gain and increased blood sugar levels. It is important to be mindful of portion sizes and to eat regular, balanced meals throughout the day. This can help prevent blood sugar spikes and crashes, which can be particularly challenging for older adults to manage.

Physical activity is another critical component of diabetes management. Regular exercise helps improve insulin sensitivity, lower blood sugar levels, and maintain a healthy weight. For individuals over 60, it is important to choose activities that are safe and appropriate for their fitness level. Walking, swimming, and gentle yoga are excellent options that provide cardiovascular benefits without putting excessive strain on the joints. It is always advisable to consult with a healthcare provider before starting a new exercise regimen, especially for those with existing health conditions.

Medications and insulin therapy may also be necessary for managing diabetes in older adults. It is important to work closely with a healthcare provider to determine the most appropriate treatment plan. Regular monitoring of blood sugar levels is essential to ensure that medications and lifestyle changes are effectively managing the condition. Additionally, older adults should be aware of the potential side effects of diabetes medications and how they may interact with other medications they are taking.

Managing diabetes after 60 also involves being vigilant about potential complications. Regular check-ups with healthcare providers, including eye exams, foot exams, and screenings for kidney function, are essential for early detection and management of complications. It is also important to stay informed about the latest advancements in diabetes care and to seek support from diabetes education programs and support groups.

In conclusion, understanding diabetes after 60 involves recognizing the physiological changes that occur with age and how they impact diabetes management. A well-balanced diet, regular physical activity, and appropriate medical care are essential components of managing diabetes and maintaining overall health. By making informed choices and working closely with healthcare providers, individuals over 60 can effectively manage their diabetes and enjoy a healthy, fulfilling life.

1.1 The impact of aging on diabetes

As we age, our bodies undergo a myriad of changes that can significantly impact the management of diabetes, particularly for those over the age of 60. Understanding these physiological changes is crucial for effective diabetes management and maintaining overall health. One of the most significant changes that occur with aging is a decrease in insulin sensitivity. Insulin is a hormone produced by the pancreas that helps regulate blood sugar levels by facilitating the uptake of glucose into cells for energy. As we age, our cells become less responsive to insulin, a condition known as insulin resistance. This means that the body needs to produce more insulin to achieve the same effect, which can strain the pancreas and eventually lead to its dysfunction. Insulin resistance is a key factor in the development of type 2 diabetes and can make blood sugar levels more difficult to control in older adults.

In addition to decreased insulin sensitivity, aging is also associated with altered metabolic rates. Metabolism refers to the chemical processes that occur within the body to maintain life, including the conversion of food into energy. As we age, our basal metabolic rate (BMR) – the number of calories our bodies need to perform basic functions at rest – tends to decrease. This reduction in BMR can lead to weight gain if caloric intake is not adjusted accordingly. Excess weight, particularly around the abdomen, is a major risk factor for insulin resistance and type 2 diabetes. Therefore, it is essential for older adults to be mindful of their caloric intake and engage in regular physical activity to maintain a healthy weight and support metabolic health.

Another important consideration is the impact of aging on muscle mass and strength. Sarcopenia, the age-related loss of muscle mass and function, is a common condition among older adults. Muscle tissue plays a critical role in glucose metabolism, as it is one of the primary sites for glucose uptake and storage. The loss of muscle mass can impair the body's ability to regulate blood sugar levels, making diabetes management more challenging. Resistance training and other forms of physical exercise can help preserve muscle mass and improve insulin sensitivity, making them valuable components of a diabetes management plan for older adults.

Aging also affects the function of the pancreas, the organ responsible for producing insulin. Over time, the beta cells in the pancreas that produce insulin may become less efficient or decrease in number, leading to reduced insulin production. This decline in pancreatic function can exacerbate the challenges of managing diabetes in older adults. Additionally, the liver, which plays a key role in glucose regulation by storing and releasing glucose as needed, may also experience age-related changes that affect its ability to maintain stable blood sugar levels.

The cardiovascular system is another area where aging can have a significant impact on diabetes management. Older adults are at an increased risk of developing cardiovascular diseases, such as hypertension (high blood pressure), atherosclerosis (hardening of the arteries), and heart disease. These conditions can complicate diabetes management and increase the risk of diabetes-related complications. For example, hypertension can damage blood vessels and reduce blood flow to vital organs, making it more difficult to control blood sugar levels and increasing the risk of complications such as diabetic neuropathy (nerve damage) and nephropathy (kidney damage).

Cognitive function can also be affected by aging, and this can have implications for diabetes management. Older adults may experience memory decline, reduced cognitive flexibility, and slower processing speeds, which can make it more challenging to adhere to complex diabetes management regimens. This includes remembering to take medications, monitoring blood sugar levels, and making appropriate dietary choices. Providing education and support to help older adults develop simple and effective diabetes management routines can be beneficial in addressing these cognitive challenges.

Furthermore, aging can affect the body's ability to sense and respond to hypoglycemia (low blood sugar). Hypoglycemia is a common concern for individuals with diabetes, particularly those on insulin or certain oral medications. As we age, the symptoms of hypoglycemia, such as shakiness, sweating, and confusion, may become less pronounced or more difficult to recognize. This can increase the risk of severe hypoglycemic episodes, which can be dangerous and require immediate medical attention. It is important for older adults with diabetes to work closely with their healthcare providers to monitor their blood sugar levels and adjust their treatment plans as needed to minimize the risk of hypoglycemia.

In addition to these physiological changes, older adults may also face social and environmental factors that can impact diabetes management. For example, limited mobility, social isolation, and financial constraints can make it more difficult to access healthy foods, engage in physical activity, and obtain necessary medical care. Addressing these barriers through community resources, social support networks, and tailored healthcare interventions can help older adults better manage their diabetes and maintain their quality of life.

Research and case studies provide valuable insights into the impact of aging on diabetes management. For instance, a study published in the Journal of Gerontology found that older adults with diabetes who engaged in regular physical activity had better blood sugar control, improved cardiovascular health, and a lower risk of diabetes-related complications compared to those who were sedentary. Another study in the journal Diabetes Care highlighted the importance of individualized dietary interventions for older adults with diabetes, emphasizing the need for balanced meals that provide adequate nutrition while managing blood sugar levels.

Case studies of older adults with diabetes also illustrate the diverse challenges and strategies for managing the condition. For example, one case study described an 80-year-old woman with type 2 diabetes who successfully improved her blood sugar control through a combination of dietary changes, increased physical activity, and regular monitoring of her blood sugar levels. With the support of her healthcare team, she was able to reduce her reliance on medication and achieve better overall health.

In conclusion, the impact of aging on diabetes is multifaceted, involving changes in insulin sensitivity, metabolic rates, muscle mass, pancreatic function, cardiovascular health, cognitive function, and the body's response to hypoglycemia. Understanding these changes and their implications for diabetes management is essential for older adults and their healthcare providers. By adopting a holistic approach that includes regular physical activity, balanced nutrition, medication management, and social support, older adults can effectively manage their diabetes and maintain their health and well-being.

1.2 Dietary principles for managing diabetes

Dietary principles for managing diabetes are crucial for maintaining healthy blood sugar levels, especially for individuals over the age of 60. As we age, our bodies undergo various physiological changes that can impact how we manage diabetes. One of the foundational dietary guidelines for managing diabetes is carbohydrate counting. Carbohydrates have a significant impact on blood sugar levels because they are broken down into glucose, which enters the bloodstream. For individuals with diabetes, it is essential to monitor carbohydrate intake to prevent spikes in blood sugar levels. Carbohydrate counting involves keeping track of the number of grams of carbohydrates consumed in each meal and snack. This method helps individuals make informed food choices and maintain stable blood sugar levels throughout the day. For example, a typical meal plan might include 45-60 grams of carbohydrates per meal and 15-30 grams per snack. It is important to note that not all carbohydrates are created equal. Simple carbohydrates, such as those found in sugary foods and beverages, can cause rapid spikes in blood sugar levels, while complex carbohydrates, such as those found in whole grains, fruits, and vegetables, are digested more slowly and have a more gradual impact on blood sugar levels.

Another important consideration in managing diabetes through diet is the glycemic index (GI). The glycemic index is a ranking system that measures how quickly a carbohydrate-containing food raises blood sugar levels. Foods with a high glycemic index, such as white bread and sugary cereals, cause rapid increases in blood sugar levels, while foods with a low glycemic index, such as whole grains and legumes, have a slower and more gradual impact on blood sugar levels. Incorporating low glycemic index foods into the diet can help individuals with diabetes maintain more stable blood sugar levels. For example, swapping white rice for brown rice or choosing whole grain bread instead of white bread can make a significant difference in blood sugar management. Additionally, pairing high glycemic index foods with protein or healthy fats can help slow down the absorption of glucose and prevent blood sugar spikes.

Fiber is another essential component of a diabetic diet. Dietary fiber, found in fruits, vegetables, whole grains, and legumes, plays a crucial role in blood sugar management. Fiber slows down the digestion and absorption of carbohydrates, leading to a more gradual rise in blood sugar levels. It also helps improve insulin sensitivity, which is particularly important for individuals with type 2 diabetes. A high-fiber diet can also aid in weight management, which is often a concern for individuals with diabetes. For example, incorporating fiber-rich foods such as oatmeal, beans, and leafy greens into meals can help individuals feel fuller for longer and reduce overall calorie intake. Research has shown that individuals who consume a high-fiber diet have better blood sugar control and lower levels of HbA1c, a marker of long-term blood sugar levels.

In addition to carbohydrate counting, glycemic index considerations, and fiber intake, portion control is a key aspect of managing diabetes through diet. Eating large portions can lead to excessive calorie intake and weight gain, which can negatively impact blood sugar levels and overall health. It is important for individuals with diabetes to be mindful of portion sizes and avoid overeating. Using smaller plates, measuring food portions, and paying attention to hunger and fullness cues can help individuals maintain appropriate portion sizes. For example, a balanced meal might include a palm-sized portion of protein, a fist-sized portion of vegetables, a cupped hand-sized portion of whole grains, and a thumb-sized portion of healthy fats.

Hydration is another important factor in managing diabetes. Staying well-hydrated helps the body function properly and can aid in blood sugar control. Dehydration can lead to higher blood sugar levels and increase the risk of complications. It is recommended that individuals with diabetes drink plenty of water throughout the day and limit their intake of sugary beverages, which can cause blood sugar spikes. For example, replacing sugary sodas with water or herbal tea can help individuals stay hydrated and maintain stable blood sugar levels.

Incorporating healthy fats into the diet is also important for individuals with diabetes. Healthy fats, such as those found in avocados, nuts, seeds, and olive oil, can help improve insulin sensitivity and reduce inflammation. These fats can also help individuals feel fuller for longer and reduce overall calorie intake. It is important to choose healthy fats over unhealthy fats, such as those found in fried foods and processed snacks, which can contribute to weight gain and negatively impact blood sugar levels. For example, adding a handful of nuts to a salad or using olive oil for cooking can provide healthy fats that support blood sugar management.

Protein is another essential component of a diabetic diet. Protein helps stabilize blood sugar levels by slowing down the absorption of carbohydrates and promoting satiety. Including a source of lean protein, such as chicken, fish, tofu, or beans, in each meal can help individuals with diabetes maintain stable blood sugar levels and prevent overeating. For example, a balanced meal might include grilled chicken breast, quinoa, and a side of steamed vegetables.

Meal timing and frequency are also important considerations for managing diabetes. Eating regular meals and snacks throughout the day can help prevent blood sugar fluctuations and maintain energy levels. Skipping meals or going long periods without eating can lead to low blood sugar levels, which can be dangerous for individuals with diabetes. It is recommended to eat three balanced meals and two to three snacks per day to maintain stable blood sugar levels. For example, a typical meal plan might include breakfast, a mid-morning snack, lunch, an afternoon snack, dinner, and an evening snack.

In addition to these dietary principles, it is important for individuals with diabetes to work closely with their healthcare team to develop a personalized meal plan that meets their specific needs and preferences. Regular monitoring of blood sugar levels, along with adjustments to the diet and medication as needed, can help individuals achieve optimal blood sugar control and overall health.

In conclusion, managing diabetes through diet involves a combination of carbohydrate counting, glycemic index considerations, fiber intake, portion control, hydration, healthy fats, protein, and meal timing. By following these dietary principles, individuals with diabetes can maintain stable blood sugar levels, improve insulin sensitivity, and reduce the risk of complications. It is important to remember that each individual's needs and preferences are unique, and working with a healthcare team to develop a personalized meal plan is essential for achieving optimal health and well-being.

1.3 Creating a daily meal structure

Creating a daily meal structure is a pivotal aspect of managing diabetes effectively, especially for individuals over 60. As we age, our bodies undergo numerous physiological changes that can impact how we process and respond to food. Therefore, establishing a consistent and balanced meal routine is essential for maintaining stable blood sugar levels and overall health. This subchapter will delve into the intricacies of structuring daily meals, offering practical tips, sample meal plans, and insights into timing and portion control for breakfast, lunch, dinner, and snacks.

The foundation of a well-structured daily meal plan for diabetes management lies in understanding the importance of regular eating patterns. Skipping meals or having irregular eating times can lead to fluctuations in blood sugar levels, making it harder to maintain control. For those over 60, who may already be dealing with the natural decline in insulin sensitivity, this can be particularly challenging. Therefore, it is crucial to establish a routine that includes three main meals and two to three snacks spaced evenly throughout the day. This approach helps to prevent large spikes and drops in blood sugar levels, providing a steady source of energy and nutrients.

Breakfast is often considered the most important meal of the day, and for good reason. After a night of fasting, your body needs fuel to kickstart your metabolism and stabilize blood sugar levels. A balanced breakfast should include a combination of complex carbohydrates, lean protein, and healthy fats. For example, a spinach and feta omelette paired with a slice of whole-grain toast and a small serving of fresh fruit can provide a nutritious start to the day. Alternatively, a bowl of cinnamon apple oatmeal topped with a handful of nuts offers a hearty and satisfying option. Including protein and fiber in your breakfast helps to slow down the absorption of glucose, preventing rapid spikes in blood sugar levels.

Moving on to lunch, it is essential to continue the trend of balanced meals that provide sustained energy. A well-rounded lunch should include a variety of vegetables, a source of lean protein, and whole grains. For instance, a quinoa and black bean salad with a side of grilled chicken offers a nutrient-dense meal that is both filling and blood sugar-friendly. Another option could be a Mediterranean chickpea wrap loaded with fresh vegetables and a light dressing. The key is to incorporate a mix of macronutrients that work together to keep blood sugar levels stable throughout the afternoon.

Dinner should be the final main meal of the day, and it is important to keep it balanced yet light enough to avoid discomfort during the night. A good dinner option could be baked salmon with dill yogurt sauce, accompanied by a side of roasted vegetables and a small portion of quinoa. This meal provides a healthy dose of omega-3 fatty acids, fiber, and protein, all of which are beneficial for blood sugar control. Another example could be a vegetable stir-fry with tofu, served over a bed of brown rice. This dish is not only quick and easy to prepare but also packed with nutrients that support overall health.

In addition to the three main meals, incorporating snacks into your daily routine can help to prevent blood sugar dips between meals. Snacks should be small and nutrient-dense, providing a quick source of energy without causing a significant rise in blood sugar levels. Some healthy snack options include a handful of almonds, a piece of fruit with a small serving of cheese, or a cup of Greek yogurt with a sprinkle of chia seeds. These snacks offer a good balance of protein, healthy fats, and carbohydrates, making them ideal for keeping blood sugar levels stable.

Timing and portion control are also critical components of a successful daily meal structure. Eating meals and snacks at regular intervals helps to maintain a consistent blood sugar level, reducing the risk of hyperglycemia or hypoglycemia. It is generally recommended to eat every 3 to 4 hours, starting with breakfast within an hour of waking up. Portion control is equally important, as overeating can lead to weight gain and increased blood sugar levels. Using smaller plates, measuring portions, and being mindful of serving sizes can help to prevent overeating and ensure that you are consuming the right amount of food for your body's needs.

Research has shown that individuals who follow a structured meal plan with consistent timing and portion control experience better blood sugar management and overall health outcomes. For example, a study published in the journal "Diabetes Care" found that older adults with type 2 diabetes who adhered to a regular meal schedule and practiced portion control had significantly lower HbA1c levels compared to those who did not. This highlights the importance of creating a daily meal structure that supports stable blood sugar levels and promotes long-term health.

In conclusion, creating a daily meal structure is a vital aspect of managing diabetes after 60. By establishing regular eating patterns, incorporating balanced meals and snacks, and paying attention to timing and portion control, you can effectively manage your blood sugar levels and improve your overall well-being. Remember, the key is to find a routine that works for you and stick to it consistently. With the right approach, you can take charge of your health and enjoy a fulfilling and healthy life.

2. The essentials of a diabetic diet

A diabetic diet is a crucial aspect of managing diabetes, especially for seniors who may face additional health challenges due to aging. Understanding the essentials of a diabetic diet involves knowing which foods to prioritize and which to limit, as well as how to read nutrition labels, understand the glycemic index, and create balanced meals that help manage blood sugar levels effectively. The first step in adopting a diabetic diet is to focus on whole, unprocessed foods. These include fresh vegetables, fruits, whole grains, lean proteins, and healthy fats. Vegetables such as leafy greens, broccoli, and bell peppers are low in calories and high in fiber, which helps in controlling blood sugar levels. Fruits, although they contain natural sugars, can be consumed in moderation, especially those with a low glycemic index like berries, apples, and pears. Whole grains such as quinoa, brown rice, and oats are preferable over refined grains because they have a lower glycemic index and provide more nutrients and fiber.

Lean proteins are essential for maintaining muscle mass and overall health, particularly in seniors. Sources of lean protein include chicken, turkey, fish, tofu, and legumes. Fish, especially fatty fish like salmon and mackerel, are rich in omega-3 fatty acids, which have been shown to reduce inflammation and improve heart health. Healthy fats, such as those found in avocados, nuts, seeds, and olive oil, should also be included in a diabetic diet. These fats can help improve cholesterol levels and provide a sense of satiety, which can prevent overeating. On the other hand, certain foods should be limited or avoided altogether. These include sugary beverages, processed snacks, white bread, pastries, and high-fat meats. Sugary drinks like soda and fruit juices can cause rapid spikes in blood sugar levels and provide little to no nutritional value. Processed snacks and baked goods often contain trans fats and added sugars, which can contribute to weight gain and increase the risk of heart disease.

Reading nutrition labels is an essential skill for anyone managing diabetes. Nutrition labels provide information on the serving size, calories, and nutrient content of a food item. When reading labels, it is important to pay attention to the total carbohydrates, dietary fiber, sugars, and added sugars. Total carbohydrates include all types of carbohydrates in the food, including sugars and fiber. Dietary fiber is beneficial because it slows the absorption of sugar into the bloodstream, helping to prevent blood sugar spikes. Sugars include both natural and added sugars, but it is the added sugars that should be minimized. The ingredient list can also provide valuable information. Ingredients are listed in order of quantity, so if sugar or high-fructose corn syrup is one of the first ingredients, it is best to avoid that product.

Understanding the glycemic index (GI) is another important aspect of managing diabetes. The glycemic index measures how quickly a carbohydrate-containing food raises blood sugar levels. Foods with a high GI, such as white bread and sugary cereals, cause rapid spikes in blood sugar, while foods with a low GI, such as lentils and non-starchy vegetables, cause a slower, more gradual increase. Choosing low-GI foods can help maintain stable blood sugar levels and reduce the risk of complications associated with diabetes. However, it is important to consider the overall nutritional value of a food, not just its GI. For example, some high-GI foods, like watermelon, are still nutritious and can be included in a balanced diet in moderation.

Creating balanced meals is key to managing diabetes effectively. A balanced meal should include a combination of carbohydrates, protein, and healthy fats. Carbohydrates should come from whole grains, vegetables, and fruits, while protein can come from lean meats, fish, tofu, or legumes. Healthy fats can be added through nuts, seeds, avocados, or olive oil. Portion control is also important, as eating large portions can lead to weight gain and make blood sugar management more difficult. Using smaller plates, measuring portions, and being mindful of hunger and fullness cues can help with portion control.

In addition to these dietary principles, staying hydrated and being physically active are important components of managing diabetes. Drinking plenty of water helps to keep the body hydrated and can aid in the regulation of blood sugar levels. Physical activity helps to improve insulin sensitivity, allowing the body to use insulin more effectively. Seniors should aim for at least 150 minutes of moderate-intensity aerobic activity, such as walking or swimming, per week, along with muscle-strengthening activities on two or more days per week.

In summary, the essentials of a diabetic diet for seniors involve prioritizing whole, unprocessed foods, limiting sugary and processed items, reading nutrition labels, understanding the glycemic index, and creating balanced meals. By following these principles, seniors can effectively manage their blood sugar levels, maintain a healthy weight, and reduce the risk of complications associated with diabetes. Empowering oneself with knowledge and making informed food choices are crucial steps in taking control of one's health and leading a fulfilling life with diabetes.

2.1 Understanding the glycemic index

The glycemic index (GI) is a critical concept for anyone managing diabetes, particularly for seniors who need to be vigilant about their blood sugar levels. The GI is a ranking system that measures how quickly carbohydrates in food are converted into glucose in the bloodstream. Foods are scored on a scale from 0 to 100, with pure glucose assigned a value of 100. Understanding the glycemic index is essential because it helps you make informed decisions about which foods to include in your diet to maintain stable blood sugar levels, which is crucial for managing diabetes effectively.

To begin with, foods with a high glycemic index (70 and above) cause a rapid spike in blood sugar levels. These include items like white bread, sugary cereals, and certain fruits like watermelon. On the other hand, foods with a low glycemic index (55 and below) are digested and absorbed more slowly, leading to a gradual rise in blood sugar levels. Examples of low-GI foods include whole grains, legumes, and most vegetables. Medium-GI foods fall between 56 and 69 and include items like whole wheat bread and brown rice.

One of the most significant benefits of consuming low-GI foods is that they help in maintaining a steady blood sugar level, which is particularly important for seniors who may have other health conditions that can be exacerbated by fluctuating glucose levels. For instance, a study published in the American Journal of Clinical Nutrition found that a low-GI diet improved glycemic control in people with type 2 diabetes. This is particularly relevant for seniors, as the body's ability to regulate blood sugar can decline with age.

Moreover, low-GI foods are often rich in fiber, which has additional health benefits. Fiber helps in digestion, prevents constipation, and can lower cholesterol levels, reducing the risk of heart disease—a common concern for older adults. For example, legumes like lentils and chickpeas are not only low-GI but also high in fiber and protein, making them excellent choices for a diabetic diet.

It's also important to consider the glycemic load (GL), which takes into account the quantity of carbohydrates in a serving of food along with its GI. The glycemic load provides a more accurate picture of how a particular food will affect blood sugar levels. For example, watermelon has a high GI but a low GL because it contains relatively few carbohydrates per serving. This means that while it can cause a rapid increase in blood sugar, the overall effect is minimal due to the small amount of carbohydrates.

Practical application of the glycemic index involves making informed food choices. For breakfast, instead of opting for high-GI sugary cereals, you could choose oatmeal topped with berries. Oatmeal has a low GI, and the berries add natural sweetness without causing a rapid spike in blood sugar. For lunch, a quinoa and black bean salad is an excellent choice. Quinoa has a low GI, and black beans are rich in fiber and protein, making this meal both nutritious and satisfying.

When it comes to dinner, consider dishes like grilled salmon with a side of roasted vegetables. Salmon is a protein-rich food with no carbohydrates, so it doesn't affect blood sugar levels. The roasted vegetables, if chosen wisely, can be low-GI options like broccoli, cauliflower, and Brussels sprouts, providing a balanced and nutritious meal.

Snacks can also be tailored to fit a low-GI diet. Instead of reaching for a bag of chips, consider a handful of nuts or a piece of fruit like an apple or pear. These options are not only low-GI but also provide essential nutrients that contribute to overall health.

Incorporating low-GI foods into your diet doesn't mean you have to give up all your favorite foods. It's about making smarter choices and understanding how different foods affect your blood sugar levels. For instance, if you love pasta, opt for whole grain or legume-based pasta instead of the traditional white pasta. These alternatives have a lower GI and are also higher in fiber and protein.

It's also worth noting that the way food is prepared can affect its glycemic index. Cooking methods that break down the structure of food, such as boiling or mashing, can increase the GI. For example, mashed potatoes have a higher GI than whole boiled potatoes. Therefore, choosing cooking methods that preserve the food's structure, like steaming or grilling, can help maintain a lower GI.

Understanding the glycemic index is not just about managing diabetes; it's about adopting a healthier lifestyle. By choosing low-GI foods, you can improve your overall health, reduce the risk of heart disease, and maintain a healthy weight. This is particularly important for seniors, as maintaining a healthy weight can help manage other age-related conditions like arthritis and high blood pressure.

In conclusion, the glycemic index is a valuable tool for anyone managing diabetes, especially seniors. By understanding and applying the principles of the glycemic index, you can make informed food choices that help maintain stable blood sugar levels, improve overall health, and enhance your quality of life. Remember, it's not about making drastic changes but about making smarter choices that fit into your lifestyle. With the right knowledge and tools, managing diabetes can be a manageable and rewarding journey.

2.2 Reading and interpreting nutrition labels

Understanding nutrition labels is an essential skill for anyone managing diabetes, especially for those over 60 who may be new to this aspect of dietary management. Nutrition labels provide a wealth of information that can help you make informed choices about the foods you consume, directly impacting your blood sugar levels and overall health. This subchapter will delve into the intricacies of reading and interpreting these labels, focusing on key nutrients such as carbohydrates, sugars, fiber, and fats, which play crucial roles in diabetes management. By mastering the art of reading nutrition labels, you can take control of your diet and make healthier choices at the grocery store, ensuring that your meals are balanced and conducive to maintaining stable blood sugar levels.

The first step in understanding nutrition labels is to familiarize yourself with the layout and the various components that make up the label. Typically, a nutrition label includes information on serving size, calories, and a breakdown of macronutrients such as carbohydrates, proteins, and fats. It also provides details on specific nutrients like fiber, sugars, sodium, and various vitamins and minerals. For individuals managing diabetes, the most critical sections to focus on are the total carbohydrates, dietary fiber, and sugars, as these directly influence blood glucose levels.

Carbohydrates are the primary nutrient that affects blood sugar levels, so it's essential to pay close attention to the total carbohydrate content on the nutrition label. This includes all forms of carbohydrates, such as sugars, starches, and fiber. When reading the label, note the serving size and the total carbohydrates per serving. It's important to remember that the serving size listed on the label may not be the same as the portion you typically consume. For example, if a serving size is one cup but you usually eat two cups, you need to double the carbohydrate content to get an accurate picture of your intake.

Sugars, both natural and added, are another crucial component to monitor. Natural sugars are found in fruits, vegetables, and dairy products, while added sugars are those that are incorporated during processing or preparation. The American Heart Association recommends that women limit their intake of added sugars to no more than 25 grams per day and men to no more than 36 grams per day. For individuals with diabetes, it's even more critical to minimize added sugars to prevent spikes in blood glucose levels. When reading nutrition labels, look for terms like "sucrose," "glucose," "high fructose corn syrup," and "honey," which indicate the presence of added sugars.

Dietary fiber is a beneficial nutrient for managing diabetes, as it helps slow the absorption of sugar into the bloodstream, preventing rapid spikes in blood glucose levels. Foods high in fiber, such as whole grains, fruits, vegetables, and legumes, are excellent choices for a diabetic diet. When reading nutrition labels, aim for foods that contain at least 3 grams of fiber per serving. The recommended daily intake of fiber is 25 grams for women and 38 grams for men, but most people fall short of this target. Incorporating high-fiber foods into your diet can help you meet these recommendations and improve blood sugar control.

Fats are another important component to consider when reading nutrition labels. While fats do not directly affect blood sugar levels, they play a significant role in overall health and can influence the risk of developing complications related to diabetes, such as heart disease. There are different types of fats, including saturated fats, trans fats, and unsaturated fats. Saturated and trans fats are considered unhealthy fats and should be limited, as they can raise cholesterol levels and increase the risk of heart disease. Unsaturated fats, found in foods like avocados, nuts, seeds, and olive oil, are healthier options that can support heart health. When reading nutrition labels, aim for foods that contain low levels of saturated and trans fats and higher levels of unsaturated fats.

Sodium is another nutrient to monitor, as high sodium intake can contribute to high blood pressure, a common complication in individuals with diabetes. The American Heart Association recommends limiting sodium intake to no more than 2,300 milligrams per day, with an ideal limit of 1,500 milligrams for most adults, especially those with high blood pressure. When reading nutrition labels, look for foods with lower sodium content and be mindful of serving sizes, as sodium can add up quickly if you're not careful.

In addition to understanding the specific nutrients on the nutrition label, it's also important to be aware of the ingredient list. Ingredients are listed in descending order by weight, so the first few ingredients make up the majority of the product. Look for whole, minimally processed ingredients and avoid products with long lists of artificial additives, preservatives, and unrecognizable ingredients. For example, if you're choosing a bread, look for one where whole grain or whole wheat is the first ingredient, rather than enriched flour or sugar.

To illustrate the importance of reading and interpreting nutrition labels, let's consider a case study of a 65-year-old woman named Mary who was recently diagnosed with type 2 diabetes. Mary loves snacking on granola bars and often chooses them as a quick and convenient option. However, after learning how to read nutrition labels, she discovered that her favorite granola bars contained high levels of added sugars and low levels of fiber, making them a poor choice for managing her blood sugar levels. By carefully reading the labels, Mary was able to find a healthier alternative with lower sugar content and higher fiber, which helped her maintain more stable blood glucose levels throughout the day.

Another example is John, a 70-year-old man who enjoys eating canned soups for lunch. After attending a diabetes education class, John learned about the importance of monitoring sodium intake. He started reading the nutrition labels on his favorite soups and was shocked to find that many of them contained over 1,000 milligrams of sodium per serving. By switching to low-sodium options and paying attention to portion sizes, John was able to significantly reduce his sodium intake, which helped lower his blood pressure and reduce his risk of heart disease.

Research also supports the benefits of reading and interpreting nutrition labels for diabetes management. A study published in the Journal of the Academy of Nutrition and Dietetics found that individuals who frequently read nutrition labels had better dietary habits and were more likely to consume a diet rich in fruits, vegetables, and whole grains. These individuals also had lower intakes of added sugars and unhealthy fats, which are critical for managing diabetes and reducing the risk of complications.

In conclusion, reading and interpreting nutrition labels is a vital skill for anyone managing diabetes, particularly for seniors who may be new to this aspect of dietary management. By understanding the layout of nutrition labels and focusing on key nutrients such as carbohydrates, sugars, fiber, and fats, you can make informed choices that support stable blood sugar levels and overall health. Paying attention to serving sizes, ingredient lists, and specific nutrient content can help you select healthier options at the grocery store and create balanced meals that align with your dietary goals. Empower yourself with the knowledge to read nutrition labels effectively, and take control of your diabetes management with confidence and ease.

2.3 Creating balanced meals

Creating balanced meals is a cornerstone of managing diabetes effectively, especially for those over 60 who are new to this dietary approach. Understanding how to assemble meals that support blood sugar regulation is crucial, as it can significantly impact overall health and well-being. A balanced meal typically includes a combination of macronutrients—carbohydrates, proteins, and fats—along with essential vitamins and minerals. The goal is to create meals that provide sustained energy, prevent blood sugar spikes, and promote satiety.

One of the first steps in creating balanced meals is understanding portion control. For seniors, portion sizes can be particularly important as metabolism slows down with age, and the body's ability to process certain nutrients changes. Using tools like measuring cups, food scales, and visual cues (such as comparing portion sizes to everyday objects) can help ensure that portions are appropriate. For example, a serving of protein should be about the size of a deck of cards, while a serving of carbohydrates might be the size of a tennis ball.

Breakfast, often touted as the most important meal of the day, sets the tone for blood sugar management. A balanced breakfast might include a combination of high-fiber carbohydrates, lean protein, and healthy fats. For instance, a spinach and feta omelette paired with a slice of whole-grain toast and a side of mixed berries provides a well-rounded start to the day. The fiber in the whole-grain toast and berries helps slow the absorption of sugar, while the protein in the omelette promotes satiety and helps maintain muscle mass, which is particularly important for seniors.

Lunch should continue the trend of balanced eating. A quinoa and black bean salad, for example, offers a mix of complex carbohydrates, plant-based protein, and healthy fats. Quinoa is a whole grain that provides fiber and essential amino acids, while black beans are rich in protein and fiber. Adding a variety of colorful vegetables, such as bell peppers, tomatoes, and cucumbers, not only enhances the nutritional profile but also adds antioxidants that support overall health. A light dressing made with olive oil and lemon juice can provide healthy fats and a burst of flavor without adding unnecessary sugars or unhealthy fats.

Dinner often serves as the main meal of the day and should be both satisfying and balanced. A dish like grilled salmon with a side of roasted vegetables and a small serving of quinoa can be an excellent choice. Salmon is rich in omega-3 fatty acids, which have been shown to reduce inflammation and support heart health—an important consideration for those with diabetes. Roasted vegetables, such as Brussels sprouts, carrots, and zucchini, provide fiber, vitamins, and minerals, while quinoa adds a source of complex carbohydrates and additional protein.

Snacks play a crucial role in maintaining blood sugar levels throughout the day. Opting for nutrient-dense snacks can prevent blood sugar dips and spikes. A handful of nuts, such as almonds or walnuts, offers healthy fats and protein, making them a great option for a mid-morning or afternoon snack. Greek yogurt with a sprinkle of chia seeds and a few slices of fresh fruit can also be a satisfying and balanced snack, providing protein, fiber, and a touch of natural sweetness.

Regular meal timing is another important aspect of managing diabetes. Eating at consistent intervals helps maintain stable blood sugar levels and prevents the extreme highs and lows that can occur with irregular eating patterns. For seniors, this might mean having three main meals and two to three smaller snacks throughout the day. It's also beneficial to avoid long periods of fasting, as this can lead to overeating and subsequent blood sugar spikes.

Incorporating a variety of foods into your diet not only ensures a wide range of nutrients but also keeps meals interesting and enjoyable. Experimenting with different recipes and ingredients can help prevent dietary boredom and encourage adherence to a diabetic-friendly eating plan. For example, trying new grains like farro or barley, or incorporating different types of fish, such as mackerel or sardines, can add variety and nutritional benefits.

Research supports the importance of a balanced diet in managing diabetes. Studies have shown that diets rich in whole grains, lean proteins, healthy fats, and a variety of fruits and vegetables can improve blood sugar control and reduce the risk of diabetes-related complications. For instance, a study published in the journal "Diabetes Care" found that individuals who followed a Mediterranean-style diet, which emphasizes whole foods and healthy fats, had better glycemic control and lower rates of cardiovascular disease.

Case studies also highlight the benefits of balanced meals for seniors with diabetes. One such case involved a 65-year-old woman who struggled with high blood sugar levels despite taking medication. By working with a dietitian to create balanced meals and incorporate regular physical activity, she was able to reduce her blood sugar levels significantly and improve her overall health. Her diet included a variety of whole grains, lean proteins, and plenty of vegetables, along with regular snacks to maintain stable blood sugar levels.

In conclusion, creating balanced meals is a fundamental aspect of managing diabetes, particularly for seniors. By focusing on portion control, incorporating a variety of nutrient-dense foods, and maintaining regular meal timing, individuals can achieve better blood sugar control and improve their overall health. Whether it's a hearty breakfast, a satisfying lunch, a nutritious dinner, or a healthy snack, each meal is an opportunity to support blood sugar management and enhance quality of life. Embracing this approach can empower seniors to take charge of their health and enjoy the benefits of a well-balanced diet.

3. Easy and nutritious breakfast recipes
3.1 Almond and blueberry smoothie

Prep time: 5 min

Cook time: 0 min

Serves: 2

Ingredients

- 1 cup - Unsweetened almond milk
- 1 cup - Fresh or frozen blueberries
- 1 - Medium banana
- 1/2 cup - Greek yogurt (plain, low-fat)
- 1 tbsp - Almond butter
- 1 tbsp - Chia seeds
- 1 tsp - Honey (optional)
- 1/2 cup - Ice cubes (optional)

Method

Step 1: In a blender, combine the unsweetened almond milk, blueberries, banana, Greek yogurt, almond butter, and chia seeds.

Step 2: Blend on high speed until smooth and creamy. If the smoothie is too thick, add a little more almond milk to reach the desired consistency.

Step 3: Taste the smoothie and add honey if additional sweetness is desired. Blend again to mix well.

Step 4: If a colder smoothie is preferred, add ice cubes and blend until the ice is crushed and the smoothie is chilled.

Step 5: Pour the smoothie into two glasses and serve immediately.

Nutritional Values

Cal: 220

Carbs: 32 g

Sugar: 18 g

Protein: 9 g

Fat: 8 g

3.2 Spinach and feta omelette

Prep time: 10 min

Cook time: 10 min

Serves: 2

Ingredients

- 4 large eggs
- 1 cup fresh spinach, chopped
- 1/2 cup feta cheese, crumbled
- 1/4 cup milk (preferably low-fat)
- 1 tablespoon olive oil
- 1/4 teaspoon black pepper
- 1/4 teaspoon salt
- 1/4 teaspoon garlic powder
- 1/4 teaspoon onion powder

Method

Step 1: In a medium bowl, whisk together the eggs, milk, salt, pepper, garlic powder, and onion powder until well combined.

Step 2: Heat the olive oil in a non-stick skillet over medium heat. Add the chopped spinach and sauté for 2-3 minutes until wilted.

Step 3: Pour the egg mixture into the skillet with the spinach. Allow the eggs to cook undisturbed for about 2 minutes until they begin to set around the edges.

Step 4: Sprinkle the crumbled feta cheese evenly over one half of the omelette.

Step 5: Using a spatula, carefully fold the other half of the omelette over the cheese. Cook for an additional 2-3 minutes until the eggs are fully set and the cheese is melted.

Step 6: Slide the omelette onto a plate and cut it in half to serve.

Nutritional Values

Cal: 250

Carbs: 4 g

Sugar: 2 g

Protein: 16 g

Fat: 18 g

3.3 Cinnamon apple oatmeal

Prep time: 10 min

Cook time: 10 min

Serves: 2

Ingredients

- 1 cup - Rolled oats
- 2 cups - Water
- 1 - Medium apple, peeled, cored, and diced
- 1 tsp - Ground cinnamon
- 1 tbsp - Chia seeds
- 1 tbsp - Maple syrup (optional)
- 1/4 cup - Unsweetened almond milk
- 1/4 tsp - Vanilla extract
- Pinch - Salt

Method

Step 1: In a medium saucepan, bring the water to a boil.

Step 2: Add the rolled oats, diced apple, ground cinnamon, and a pinch of salt to the boiling water.

Step 3: Reduce the heat to low and simmer for about 5-7 minutes, stirring occasionally, until the oats are tender and the mixture has thickened.

Step 4: Stir in the chia seeds, almond milk, and vanilla extract. Cook for an additional 2 minutes.

Step 5: Remove from heat and let the oatmeal sit for a minute to thicken further.

Step 6: Divide the oatmeal into two bowls and drizzle with maple syrup if desired.

Nutritional Values

Cal: 250

Carbs: 45 g

Sugar: 12 g

Protein: 6 g

Fat: 5 g

3.4 Chia seed pudding with berries

Prep time: 10 min

Cook time: 0 min

Serves: 2

Ingredients

- 1/4 cup - chia seeds

- 1 cup - unsweetened almond milk

- 1/2 tsp - vanilla extract

- 1 tbsp - maple syrup (optional)

- 1/2 cup - mixed berries (blueberries, raspberries, strawberries)

- 1 tbsp - chopped nuts (optional)

- 1 tbsp - unsweetened shredded coconut (optional)

Method

Step 1: In a medium bowl, combine chia seeds, almond milk, vanilla extract, and maple syrup (if using). Stir well to ensure the chia seeds are evenly distributed.
Step 2: Cover the bowl and refrigerate for at least 4 hours or overnight, allowing the chia seeds to absorb the liquid and form a pudding-like consistency.
Step 3: Before serving, give the pudding a good stir to break up any clumps.
Step 4: Divide the chia seed pudding into two serving bowls.
Step 5: Top each bowl with mixed berries, chopped nuts, and shredded coconut (if using).

Nutritional Values

Cal: 180

Carbs: 20 g

Sugar: 6 g

Protein: 5 g

Fat: 9 g

3.5 Avocado toast with poached egg

Prep time: 10 min

Cook time: 5 min

Serves: 2

Ingredients

- 2 slices - Whole grain bread
- 1 - Ripe avocado
- 2 - Large eggs
- 1 tbsp - Lemon juice
- 1/4 tsp - Salt
- 1/4 tsp - Black pepper
- 1 tbsp - Chopped fresh chives (optional)
- 1 tbsp - Olive oil

Method

Step 1: Toast the whole grain bread slices until they are golden brown and crispy.

Step 2: While the bread is toasting, cut the avocado in half, remove the pit, and scoop the flesh into a bowl. Mash the avocado with a fork until smooth, then mix in the lemon juice, salt, and black pepper.

Step 3: Fill a medium-sized pot with water and bring it to a gentle simmer. Add a splash of vinegar to the water to help the eggs hold their shape.

Step 4: Crack each egg into a small bowl or ramekin. Create a gentle whirlpool in the pot using a spoon, then carefully slide each egg into the water. Poach the eggs for about 3-4 minutes, or until the whites are set but the yolks are still runny.

Step 5: Spread the mashed avocado evenly over the toasted bread slices.

Step 6: Use a slotted spoon to carefully remove the poached eggs from the water and place one egg on top of each avocado toast.

Step 7: Drizzle the olive oil over the top and sprinkle with chopped fresh chives if desired.

Nutritional Values

Cal: 350

Carbs: 30 g

Sugar: 2 g

Protein: 12 g

Fat: 22 g

3.6 Low-carb yogurt parfait

Prep time: 10 min

Cook time: 0 min

Serves: 2

Ingredients

- 1 cup - Greek yogurt (plain, unsweetened)
- 1/2 cup - Fresh berries (strawberries, blueberries, raspberries)
- 1/4 cup - Chopped nuts (almonds, walnuts, or pecans)
- 1 tbsp - Chia seeds
- 1 tsp - Vanilla extract
- 1/2 tsp - Ground cinnamon
- 1 tbsp - Unsweetened shredded coconut (optional)
- 1 tbsp - Sugar-free sweetener (optional)

Method

Step 1: In a medium bowl, mix the Greek yogurt with the vanilla extract and ground cinnamon until well combined.

Step 2: Divide the yogurt mixture evenly between two serving glasses or bowls.

Step 3: Layer the fresh berries on top of the yogurt mixture.

Step 4: Sprinkle the chopped nuts and chia seeds over the berries.

Step 5: If desired, add a sprinkle of unsweetened shredded coconut and a drizzle of sugar-free sweetener on top.

Step 6: Serve immediately or refrigerate for up to 2 hours before serving.

Nutritional Values

Cal: 220

Carbs: 12 g

Sugar: 6 g

Protein: 15 g

Fat: 14 g

3.7 Turkey and spinach breakfast burrito

Prep time: 10 min

Cook time: 10 min

Serves: 2

Ingredients

- 4 - Large eggs
- 1/4 cup - Skim milk
- 1/2 cup - Fresh spinach, chopped
- 1/2 cup - Cooked turkey breast, diced
- 1/4 cup - Low-fat shredded cheese
- 2 - Whole wheat tortillas
- 1 tbsp - Olive oil
- 1/4 tsp - Salt
- 1/4 tsp - Black pepper
- 1/4 cup - Salsa (optional)

Method

Step 1: In a medium bowl, whisk together the eggs, skim milk, salt, and black pepper until well combined.

Step 2: Heat the olive oil in a non-stick skillet over medium heat. Add the egg mixture and cook, stirring occasionally, until the eggs are scrambled and fully cooked.

Step 3: Add the chopped spinach and diced turkey breast to the skillet. Cook for an additional 2-3 minutes until the spinach is wilted and the turkey is heated through.

Step 4: Warm the whole wheat tortillas in a separate skillet or microwave. Place half of the egg mixture onto each tortilla.

Step 5: Sprinkle the low-fat shredded cheese over the egg mixture. Roll up the tortillas to form burritos.

Step 6: Serve immediately, with salsa on the side if desired.

Nutritional Values

Cal: 320

Carbs: 28 g

Sugar: 2 g

Protein: 25 g

Fat: 12 g

3.8 Cottage cheese and peach bowl

Prep time: 10 min

Cook time: 0 min

Serves: 2

Ingredients

- 1 cup - Cottage cheese (low-fat)
- 2 - Medium peaches, sliced
- 2 tbsp - Chopped walnuts
- 1 tbsp - Honey (optional)
- 1/2 tsp - Ground cinnamon
- 1/2 cup - Fresh mint leaves (optional, for garnish)

Method

Step 1: Divide the cottage cheese evenly between two bowls.

Step 2: Arrange the sliced peaches on top of the cottage cheese in each bowl.

Step 3: Sprinkle the chopped walnuts over the peaches.

Step 4: Drizzle honey over the top if using.

Step 5: Sprinkle ground cinnamon evenly over both bowls.

Step 6: Garnish with fresh mint leaves if desired.

Nutritional Values

Cal: 220

Carbs: 22 g

Sugar: 18 g

Protein: 14 g

Fat: 9 g

3.9 Buckwheat pancakes

Prep time: 10 min
Cook time: 15 min
Serves: 2

Ingredients
- 1/2 cup - Buckwheat flour
- 1/4 cup - Almond flour
- 1/2 tsp - Baking powder
- 1/4 tsp - Baking soda
- 1/4 tsp - Salt
- 1 - Large egg
- 1/2 cup - Unsweetened almond milk
- 1 tbsp - Olive oil
- 1 tsp - Vanilla extract
- 1 tbsp - Stevia or erythritol (optional)
- 1/4 cup - Fresh blueberries (optional)

Method
Step 1: In a medium bowl, whisk together the buckwheat flour, almond flour, baking powder, baking soda, and salt.
Step 2: In another bowl, beat the egg and then add the almond milk, olive oil, and vanilla extract. Mix well.
Step 3: Pour the wet ingredients into the dry ingredients and stir until just combined. If using, fold in the sweetener and fresh blueberries.
Step 4: Heat a non-stick skillet over medium heat and lightly grease it with a small amount of olive oil.
Step 5: Pour 1/4 cup of the batter onto the skillet for each pancake. Cook until bubbles form on the surface, then flip and cook until golden brown on the other side, about 2-3 minutes per side.
Step 6: Serve warm with your choice of toppings, such as fresh fruit, a dollop of Greek yogurt, or a drizzle of sugar-free syrup.

Nutritional Values
Cal: 220
Carbs: 28 g
Sugar: 2 g
Protein: 8 g
Fat: 9 g

3.10 Veggie-packed frittata

Prep time: 10 min

Cook time: 20 min

Serves: 2

Ingredients

- 4 large eggs
- 1/4 cup milk (preferably low-fat)
- 1/2 cup cherry tomatoes, halved
- 1/2 cup spinach, chopped
- 1/4 cup bell pepper, diced
- 1/4 cup red onion, finely chopped
- 1/4 cup zucchini, diced
- 1/4 cup feta cheese, crumbled
- 1 tbsp olive oil
- Salt and pepper to taste
- 1/4 tsp dried oregano

Method

Step 1: Preheat the oven to 375°F (190°C).

Step 2: In a medium bowl, whisk together the eggs, milk, salt, pepper, and dried oregano until well combined.

Step 3: Heat the olive oil in an oven-safe skillet over medium heat. Add the red onion and bell pepper, and sauté for 3-4 minutes until they begin to soften.

Step 4: Add the zucchini and cherry tomatoes to the skillet, and cook for another 2-3 minutes.

Step 5: Stir in the chopped spinach and cook until wilted, about 1-2 minutes.

Step 6: Pour the egg mixture over the vegetables in the skillet, ensuring the mixture is evenly distributed.

Step 7: Sprinkle the crumbled feta cheese on top.

Step 8: Transfer the skillet to the preheated oven and bake for 15-20 minutes, or until the frittata is set and lightly golden on top.

Step 9: Remove from the oven and let it cool slightly before slicing and serving.

Nutritional Values

Cal: 250

Carbs: 10 g

Sugar: 5 g

Protein: 18 g

Fat: 16 g

3.11 Tofu scramble with kale

Prep time: 10 min

Cook time: 10 min

Serves: 2

Ingredients

- 1 tbsp - Olive oil
- 1/2 - Medium onion, finely chopped
- 1 - Garlic clove, minced
- 1/2 - Red bell pepper, diced
- 1/2 cup - Cherry tomatoes, halved
- 1/2 tsp - Turmeric powder
- 1/2 tsp - Ground cumin
- 1/4 tsp - Paprika
- 1/4 tsp - Black pepper
- 1/2 tsp - Salt
- 1 block (200g) - Firm tofu, crumbled
- 2 cups - Fresh kale, chopped
- 1 tbsp - Nutritional yeast (optional)
- 1 tbsp - Fresh lemon juice
- 2 tbsp - Fresh parsley, chopped (optional)

Method

Step 1: Heat the olive oil in a large skillet over medium heat. Add the chopped onion and cook for 2-3 minutes until it becomes translucent.

Step 2: Add the minced garlic, diced red bell pepper, and cherry tomatoes to the skillet. Cook for another 2-3 minutes until the vegetables are tender.

Step 3: Stir in the turmeric powder, ground cumin, paprika, black pepper, and salt. Mix well to coat the vegetables with the spices.

Step 4: Add the crumbled tofu to the skillet and cook for 3-4 minutes, stirring occasionally, until the tofu is heated through and slightly golden.

Step 5: Add the chopped kale to the skillet and cook for another 2 minutes until the kale is wilted.

Step 6: If using, sprinkle the nutritional yeast over the tofu scramble and stir to combine. Add the fresh lemon juice and mix well.

Step 7: Remove the skillet from heat and garnish with fresh parsley if desired. Serve hot.

Nutritional Values

Cal: 220

Carbs: 15 g

Sugar: 4 g

Protein: 18 g

Fat: 12 g

3.12 Quinoa breakfast bowl

Prep time: 10 min

Cook time: 15 min

Serves: 2

Ingredients

- 1/2 cup - Quinoa
- 1 cup - Water
- 1/2 cup - Unsweetened almond milk
- 1/2 tsp - Ground cinnamon
- 1/4 tsp - Vanilla extract
- 1 tbsp - Chia seeds
- 1/4 cup - Fresh blueberries
- 1/4 cup - Fresh strawberries, sliced
- 1/4 cup - Sliced almonds
- 1 tbsp - Unsweetened shredded coconut
- 1 tbsp - Honey (optional)

Method

Step 1: Rinse the quinoa under cold water to remove any bitterness.

Step 2: In a medium saucepan, combine the quinoa and water. Bring to a boil over medium-high heat, then reduce the heat to low, cover, and simmer for about 15 minutes or until the water is absorbed and the quinoa is tender.

Step 3: Remove the saucepan from the heat and let it sit, covered, for 5 minutes. Fluff the quinoa with a fork.

Step 4: Stir in the almond milk, ground cinnamon, and vanilla extract. Mix well.

Step 5: Divide the quinoa mixture between two bowls.

Step 6: Top each bowl with chia seeds, blueberries, strawberries, sliced almonds, and shredded coconut.

Step 7: Drizzle with honey if desired.

Nutritional Values

Cal: 300

Carbs: 45 g

Sugar: 10 g

Protein: 10 g

Fat: 10 g

3.13 Smoked salmon and cream cheese bagel

Prep time: 10 min

Cook time: 5 min

Serves: 2

Ingredients

- 2 - Whole grain bagels
- 4 oz - Smoked salmon
- 4 tbsp - Low-fat cream cheese
- 1/2 - Red onion, thinly sliced
- 1 - Small cucumber, thinly sliced
- 1 tbsp - Capers
- 1 tbsp - Fresh dill, chopped
- 1/2 - Lemon, cut into wedges
- Pinch - Black pepper

Method

Step 1: Slice the whole grain bagels in half and toast them until they are golden brown.

Step 2: Spread 1 tablespoon of low-fat cream cheese on each half of the toasted bagels.

Step 3: Layer the smoked salmon evenly over the cream cheese on each bagel half.

Step 4: Top the smoked salmon with thinly sliced red onion and cucumber.

Step 5: Sprinkle capers and fresh dill over the top.

Step 6: Add a pinch of black pepper to taste.

Step 7: Serve each bagel half with a lemon wedge on the side for squeezing over the top.

Nutritional Values

Cal: 350

Carbs: 40 g

Sugar: 5 g

Protein: 20 g

Fat: 12 g

3.14 Nutty banana bread

Prep time: 10 min
Cook time: 50 min
Serves: 2

Ingredients
- 1 large - Ripe banana
- 1 large - Egg
- 2 tbsp - Unsweetened applesauce
- 1/4 cup - Greek yogurt
- 1/2 tsp - Vanilla extract
- 1/2 cup - Whole wheat flour
- 1/4 cup - Almond flour
- 1/4 tsp - Baking soda
- 1/4 tsp - Baking powder
- 1/4 tsp - Ground cinnamon
- 1/8 tsp - Salt
- 2 tbsp - Chopped walnuts
- 2 tbsp - Chopped almonds

Method
Step 1: Preheat your oven to 350°F (175°C). Lightly grease a small loaf pan or line it with parchment paper.
Step 2: In a medium bowl, mash the ripe banana until smooth. Add the egg, unsweetened applesauce, Greek yogurt, and vanilla extract. Mix well until all ingredients are combined.
Step 3: In another bowl, whisk together the whole wheat flour, almond flour, baking soda, baking powder, ground cinnamon, and salt.
Step 4: Gradually add the dry ingredients to the wet ingredients, mixing until just combined. Be careful not to overmix.
Step 5: Fold in the chopped walnuts and almonds.
Step 6: Pour the batter into the prepared loaf pan and spread it out evenly.
Step 7: Bake in the preheated oven for 50 minutes or until a toothpick inserted into the center comes out clean.
Step 8: Allow the nutty banana bread to cool in the pan for 10 minutes before transferring it to a wire rack to cool completely. Slice and serve.

Nutritional Values
Cal: 250
Carbs: 30 g
Sugar: 10 g
Protein: 8 g
Fat: 10 g

3.15 Sautéed mushrooms and tomatoes on toast

Prep time: 10 min

Cook time: 10 min

Serves: 2

Ingredients

- 4 slices - whole grain bread
- 1 cup - cherry tomatoes, halved
- 1 cup - button mushrooms, sliced
- 1 tbsp - olive oil
- 1 clove - garlic, minced
- 1/4 tsp - dried thyme
- 1/4 tsp - dried oregano
- Salt and pepper to taste
- 1/4 cup - fresh parsley, chopped (optional)

Method

Step 1: Toast the whole grain bread slices until they are golden brown and crispy.

Step 2: In a large skillet, heat the olive oil over medium heat. Add the minced garlic and sauté for 1 minute until fragrant.

Step 3: Add the sliced mushrooms to the skillet and cook for 5 minutes, stirring occasionally, until they start to brown.

Step 4: Add the halved cherry tomatoes to the skillet and cook for another 3-4 minutes until they are soft and slightly blistered.

Step 5: Season the mushroom and tomato mixture with dried thyme, dried oregano, salt, and pepper. Stir well to combine.

Step 6: Divide the sautéed mushrooms and tomatoes evenly over the toasted bread slices.

Step 7: Garnish with fresh chopped parsley if desired and serve immediately.

Nutritional Values

Cal: 220

Carbs: 30 g

Sugar: 5 g

Protein: 6 g

Fat: 9 g

3.16 Protein-rich breakfast bars

Prep time: 10 min
Cook time: 20 min
Serves: 2

Ingredients
- 1 cup - Rolled oats
- 1/2 cup - Protein powder (vanilla or unflavored)
- 1/4 cup - Almond butter
- 1/4 cup - Honey or agave syrup
- 1/4 cup - Chopped nuts (almonds, walnuts, or pecans)
- 1/4 cup - Unsweetened dried cranberries
- 1/4 cup - Unsweetened shredded coconut
- 1/4 cup - Dark chocolate chips (optional)
- 1/4 cup - Milk (almond, soy, or regular)
- 1 tsp - Vanilla extract
- 1/4 tsp - Salt

Method
Step 1: Preheat your oven to 350°F (175°C) and line a baking dish with parchment paper.
Step 2: In a large mixing bowl, combine the rolled oats, protein powder, chopped nuts, dried cranberries, shredded coconut, and dark chocolate chips (if using).
Step 3: In a small saucepan over low heat, melt the almond butter and honey (or agave syrup) together until smooth. Remove from heat and stir in the vanilla extract and salt.
Step 4: Pour the almond butter mixture over the dry ingredients and mix well until everything is evenly coated. Add the milk gradually to help bind the mixture together.
Step 5: Transfer the mixture to the prepared baking dish and press it down firmly to create an even layer.
Step 6: Bake in the preheated oven for 15-20 minutes, or until the edges are golden brown.
Step 7: Allow the bars to cool completely in the baking dish before cutting them into squares or bars.

Nutritional Values
Cal: 350
Carbs: 40 g
Sugar: 15 g
Protein: 20 g
Fat: 15 g

3.17 Green detox smoothie

Prep time: 10 min

Cook time: 0 min

Serves: 2

Ingredients

- 1 cup - fresh spinach
- 1 cup - kale
- 1 - medium green apple, cored and chopped
- 1 - small cucumber, peeled and chopped
- 1 - small avocado, peeled and pitted
- 1 tbsp - chia seeds
- 1 cup - unsweetened almond milk
- 1/2 cup - water
- 1 tbsp - fresh lemon juice
- 1/2 tsp - grated ginger
- 1/2 cup - ice cubes

Method

Step 1: Add the fresh spinach, kale, green apple, cucumber, and avocado to a blender.

Step 2: Add the chia seeds, unsweetened almond milk, water, fresh lemon juice, and grated ginger to the blender.

Step 3: Blend on high speed until smooth and creamy.

Step 4: Add the ice cubes and blend again until the ice is crushed and the smoothie is cold.

Step 5: Pour into two glasses and serve immediately.

Nutritional Values

Cal: 180

Carbs: 22 g

Sugar: 10 g

Protein: 4 g

Fat: 9 g

3.18 Ricotta and pear toast

Prep time: 10 min

Cook time: 5 min

Serves: 2

Ingredients

- 4 slices - Whole grain bread
- 1 cup - Ricotta cheese
- 1 - Ripe pear
- 1 tbsp - Honey (optional, for a touch of sweetness)
- 1/4 tsp - Ground cinnamon
- 1/4 cup - Chopped walnuts (optional, for added crunch)
- 1 tsp - Lemon juice

Method

Step 1: Toast the whole grain bread slices until they are golden brown and crispy.
Step 2: While the bread is toasting, wash the pear and cut it into thin slices. Drizzle the slices with lemon juice to prevent browning.
Step 3: Spread an even layer of ricotta cheese on each slice of toasted bread.
Step 4: Arrange the pear slices on top of the ricotta cheese.
Step 5: Drizzle a small amount of honey over the pear slices, if using.
Step 6: Sprinkle ground cinnamon over the top for added flavor.
Step 7: Optionally, add chopped walnuts on top for a crunchy texture.

Nutritional Values

Cal: 250

Carbs: 30 g

Sugar: 10 g

Protein: 10 g

Fat: 10 g

3.19 Southwestern tofu hash

Prep time: 10 min
Cook time: 15 min
Serves: 2

Ingredients
- 1 tbsp - Olive oil
- 1/2 - Medium red onion, diced
- 1 - Red bell pepper, diced
- 1 - Green bell pepper, diced
- 2 cloves - Garlic, minced
- 1/2 tsp - Ground cumin
- 1/2 tsp - Smoked paprika
- 1/4 tsp - Ground turmeric
- 1/4 tsp - Black pepper
- 1/2 tsp - Salt
- 1 block (200g) - Firm tofu, drained and crumbled
- 1 - Medium sweet potato, peeled and diced
- 2 tbsp - Fresh cilantro, chopped
- 1 - Avocado, sliced (optional, for serving)
- 2 tbsp - Salsa (optional, for serving)

Method
Step 1: Heat the olive oil in a large skillet over medium heat. Add the diced red onion and cook until it begins to soften, about 3 minutes.
Step 2: Add the diced red and green bell peppers to the skillet and cook for another 3-4 minutes until they start to soften.
Step 3: Add the minced garlic, ground cumin, smoked paprika, ground turmeric, black pepper, and salt. Stir well to combine and cook for 1 minute until fragrant.
Step 4: Add the crumbled tofu to the skillet, stirring to mix with the vegetables and spices. Cook for 5 minutes, stirring occasionally.
Step 5: Add the diced sweet potato to the skillet. Cover and cook for 5-7 minutes, stirring occasionally, until the sweet potato is tender.
Step 6: Remove the skillet from heat and stir in the chopped fresh cilantro.
Step 7: Serve the tofu hash warm, optionally topped with sliced avocado and salsa.

Nutritional Values
Cal: 320
Carbs: 28 g
Sugar: 6 g
Protein: 14 g
Fat: 18 g

3.20 Pumpkin spice oatmeal

Prep time: 5 min

Cook time: 10 min

Serves: 2

Ingredients

- 1 cup - rolled oats
- 2 cups - unsweetened almond milk
- 1/2 cup - pumpkin puree
- 1 tbsp - chia seeds
- 1 tsp - pumpkin pie spice
- 1/2 tsp - ground cinnamon
- 1/4 tsp - vanilla extract
- 1 tbsp - maple syrup (optional)
- 2 tbsp - chopped pecans (optional)
- 1/4 cup - fresh blueberries (optional)

Method

Step 1: In a medium saucepan, combine the rolled oats and unsweetened almond milk. Bring to a boil over medium heat.

Step 2: Reduce the heat to low and stir in the pumpkin puree, chia seeds, pumpkin pie spice, ground cinnamon, and vanilla extract.

Step 3: Cook, stirring occasionally, for about 5-7 minutes, or until the oats are tender and the mixture has thickened.

Step 4: If desired, stir in the maple syrup for added sweetness.

Step 5: Divide the oatmeal into two bowls. Top with chopped pecans and fresh blueberries if using.

Nutritional Values

Cal: 220

Carbs: 36 g

Sugar: 5 g

Protein: 6 g

Fat: 6 g

4. Wholesome lunch recipes for optimal health
4.1 Turkey and spinach stuffed peppers

Prep time: 15 min

Cook time: 30 min

Serves: 2

Ingredients

- 2 large bell peppers
- 200g ground turkey
- 1 cup fresh spinach, chopped
- 1/2 cup cooked quinoa
- 1/4 cup diced onion
- 1 clove garlic, minced
- 1/2 cup diced tomatoes
- 1/4 cup shredded mozzarella cheese
- 1 tbsp olive oil
- 1 tsp dried oregano
- 1/2 tsp salt
- 1/4 tsp black pepper

Method

Step 1: Preheat the oven to 375°F (190°C). Cut the tops off the bell peppers and remove the seeds and membranes. Set aside.

Step 2: In a large skillet, heat the olive oil over medium heat. Add the diced onion and minced garlic, and sauté until the onion is translucent, about 3-4 minutes.

Step 3: Add the ground turkey to the skillet and cook until browned, breaking it up with a spoon as it cooks, about 5-7 minutes.

Step 4: Stir in the chopped spinach, cooked quinoa, diced tomatoes, dried oregano, salt, and black pepper. Cook for an additional 2-3 minutes until the spinach is wilted and the mixture is well combined.

Step 5: Stuff each bell pepper with the turkey and spinach mixture, pressing down gently to pack the filling.

Step 6: Place the stuffed peppers in a baking dish and cover with aluminum foil. Bake in the preheated oven for 20 minutes.

Step 7: Remove the foil, sprinkle the shredded mozzarella cheese on top of each stuffed pepper, and bake for an additional 10 minutes, or until the cheese is melted and bubbly.

Step 8: Remove from the oven and let cool for a few minutes before serving.

Nutritional Values

Cal: 350

Carbs: 20 g

Sugar: 6 g

Protein: 30 g

Fat: 15 g

4.2 Quinoa and black bean salad

Prep time: 15 min
Cook time: 15 min
Serves: 2

Ingredients
- 1/2 cup - quinoa
- 1 cup - water
- 1 cup - black beans, cooked and drained
- 1/2 cup - cherry tomatoes, halved
- 1/2 cup - cucumber, diced
- 1/4 cup - red bell pepper, diced
- 1/4 cup - red onion, finely chopped
- 1/4 cup - fresh cilantro, chopped
- 1 - avocado, diced
- 2 tbsp - olive oil
- 1 tbsp - lime juice
- 1 tsp - ground cumin
- 1/2 tsp - salt
- 1/4 tsp - black pepper

Method
Step 1: Rinse the quinoa under cold water. In a medium saucepan, combine the quinoa and water. Bring to a boil, then reduce the heat to low, cover, and simmer for about 15 minutes or until the water is absorbed and the quinoa is tender. Remove from heat and let it cool.
Step 2: In a large mixing bowl, combine the black beans, cherry tomatoes, cucumber, red bell pepper, red onion, and fresh cilantro.
Step 3: Once the quinoa has cooled, add it to the mixing bowl with the vegetables and beans. Gently toss to combine.
Step 4: In a small bowl, whisk together the olive oil, lime juice, ground cumin, salt, and black pepper. Pour the dressing over the salad and toss to coat evenly.
Step 5: Gently fold in the diced avocado. Serve immediately or refrigerate for up to 2 hours to allow the flavors to meld.

Nutritional Values
Cal: 420
Carbs: 50 g
Sugar: 5 g
Protein: 12 g
Fat: 20 g

4.3 Broccoli and cheddar soup

Prep time: 15 min

Cook time: 25 min

Serves: 2

Ingredients

- 1 tablespoon - olive oil
- 1 small - onion, finely chopped
- 1 clove - garlic, minced
- 1 medium - carrot, diced
- 1 medium - celery stalk, diced
- 2 cups - broccoli florets
- 2 cups - low-sodium vegetable broth
- 1 cup - skim milk
- 1 cup - shredded low-fat cheddar cheese
- 1 tablespoon - whole wheat flour
- Salt and pepper to taste

Method

Step 1: Heat olive oil in a large pot over medium heat. Add the chopped onion, minced garlic, diced carrot, and diced celery. Sauté until the vegetables are tender, about 5 minutes.

Step 2: Add the broccoli florets and vegetable broth to the pot. Bring to a boil, then reduce the heat and let it simmer for 10 minutes, or until the broccoli is tender.

Step 3: In a small bowl, whisk together the skim milk and whole wheat flour until smooth. Gradually stir this mixture into the soup.

Step 4: Continue to cook the soup, stirring frequently, until it thickens, about 5 minutes.

Step 5: Remove the pot from heat and stir in the shredded cheddar cheese until melted and well combined. Season with salt and pepper to taste.

Step 6: Use an immersion blender to blend the soup to your desired consistency, or transfer to a blender in batches and blend until smooth.

Nutritional Values

Cal: 250

Carbs: 25 g

Sugar: 8 g

Protein: 15 g

Fat: 10 g

4.4 Grilled chicken caesar salad

Prep time: 15 min

Cook time: 10 min

Serves: 2

Ingredients

- 2 - Boneless, skinless chicken breasts
- 1 tbsp - Olive oil
- 1 tsp - Garlic powder
- 1 tsp - Dried oregano
- 1/2 tsp - Salt
- 1/4 tsp - Black pepper
- 4 cups - Romaine lettuce, chopped
- 1/4 cup - Grated Parmesan cheese
- 1/2 cup - Cherry tomatoes, halved
- 1/4 cup - Whole grain croutons
- 2 tbsp - Caesar dressing (low-fat, low-sugar)

Method

Step 1: Preheat the grill to medium-high heat.
Step 2: In a small bowl, mix olive oil, garlic powder, dried oregano, salt, and black pepper.
Step 3: Brush the chicken breasts with the olive oil mixture.
Step 4: Grill the chicken breasts for about 5 minutes on each side, or until fully cooked and no longer pink in the center.
Step 5: Remove the chicken from the grill and let it rest for a few minutes before slicing it into thin strips.
Step 6: In a large bowl, combine the chopped romaine lettuce, grated Parmesan cheese, cherry tomatoes, and whole grain croutons.
Step 7: Add the sliced grilled chicken to the salad.
Step 8: Drizzle the Caesar dressing over the salad and toss gently to combine.

Nutritional Values

Cal: 350

Carbs: 15 g

Sugar: 3 g

Protein: 35 g

Fat: 15 g

4.5 Vegetable stir-fry with tofu

Prep time: 15 min
Cook time: 15 min
Serves: 2

Ingredients
- 200g - Firm tofu, cubed
- 1 tbsp - Olive oil
- 1 - Red bell pepper, sliced
- 1 - Yellow bell pepper, sliced
- 1 - Medium carrot, julienned
- 100g - Broccoli florets
- 1 - Small zucchini, sliced
- 2 cloves - Garlic, minced
- 1 tbsp - Fresh ginger, minced
- 2 tbsp - Low-sodium soy sauce
- 1 tbsp - Rice vinegar
- 1 tsp - Sesame oil
- 1 tbsp - Sesame seeds
- 2 - Green onions, sliced
- 1/4 cup - Fresh cilantro, chopped

Method
Step 1: Heat the olive oil in a large skillet or wok over medium-high heat. Add the cubed tofu and cook until golden brown on all sides, about 5-7 minutes. Remove tofu from the skillet and set aside.
Step 2: In the same skillet, add the garlic and ginger, and sauté for 1 minute until fragrant.
Step 3: Add the red and yellow bell peppers, carrot, broccoli, and zucchini to the skillet. Stir-fry for 5-7 minutes until the vegetables are tender-crisp.
Step 4: Return the tofu to the skillet and pour in the soy sauce, rice vinegar, and sesame oil. Toss everything together to coat evenly.
Step 5: Sprinkle the sesame seeds over the stir-fry and mix well. Cook for an additional 1-2 minutes.
Step 6: Remove from heat and garnish with sliced green onions and chopped cilantro before serving.

Nutritional Values
Cal: 320
Carbs: 28 g
Sugar: 10 g
Protein: 18 g
Fat: 16 g

4.6 Mediterranean chickpea wrap

Prep time: 15 min

Cook time: 5 min

Serves: 2

Ingredients

- 1 cup - canned chickpeas, drained and rinsed
- 1/2 cup - cherry tomatoes, halved
- 1/2 cup - cucumber, diced
- 1/4 cup - red onion, finely chopped
- 1/4 cup - Kalamata olives, pitted and sliced
- 1/4 cup - feta cheese, crumbled
- 2 tbsp - fresh parsley, chopped
- 2 tbsp - extra virgin olive oil
- 1 tbsp - lemon juice
- 1 tsp - dried oregano
- 1/2 tsp - garlic powder
- Salt and pepper to taste
- 2 - whole wheat wraps

Method

Step 1: In a large bowl, combine the chickpeas, cherry tomatoes, cucumber, red onion, Kalamata olives, feta cheese, and fresh parsley.

Step 2: In a small bowl, whisk together the extra virgin olive oil, lemon juice, dried oregano, garlic powder, salt, and pepper.

Step 3: Pour the dressing over the chickpea mixture and toss to coat evenly.

Step 4: Warm the whole wheat wraps in a dry skillet over medium heat for about 1 minute on each side.

Step 5: Divide the chickpea mixture evenly between the two wraps, placing it in the center of each wrap.

Step 6: Fold in the sides of the wrap and then roll it up tightly from the bottom.

Step 7: Slice each wrap in half and serve immediately.

Nutritional Values

Cal: 400

Carbs: 45 g

Sugar: 6 g

Protein: 12 g

Fat: 18 g

4.7 Zucchini noodle caprese

Prep time: 15 min

Cook time: 5 min

Serves: 2

Ingredients

- 2 medium zucchinis - spiralized into noodles
- 1 cup - cherry tomatoes, halved
- 1/2 cup - fresh mozzarella balls, halved
- 1/4 cup - fresh basil leaves, chopped
- 2 tbsp - extra-virgin olive oil
- 1 tbsp - balsamic vinegar
- 1 clove - garlic, minced
- Salt and pepper to taste

Method

Step 1: Spiralize the zucchinis into noodles using a spiralizer or julienne peeler. Place the zucchini noodles in a large bowl.
Step 2: Add the halved cherry tomatoes, mozzarella balls, and chopped basil to the bowl with the zucchini noodles.
Step 3: In a small bowl, whisk together the extra-virgin olive oil, balsamic vinegar, minced garlic, salt, and pepper.
Step 4: Pour the dressing over the zucchini noodle mixture and toss gently to combine.
Step 5: Serve immediately or refrigerate for up to an hour before serving.

Nutritional Values

Cal: 220

Carbs: 12 g

Sugar: 7 g

Protein: 8 g

Fat: 16 g

4.8 Lentil soup with spinach

Prep time: 15 min
Cook time: 30 min
Serves: 2

Ingredients
- 1/2 cup - dried lentils, rinsed and drained
- 1 tbsp - olive oil
- 1 - medium onion, finely chopped
- 2 - garlic cloves, minced
- 1 - medium carrot, diced
- 1 - celery stalk, diced
- 4 cups - low-sodium vegetable broth
- 1 cup - fresh spinach, chopped
- 1/2 tsp - ground cumin
- 1/2 tsp - ground coriander
- 1/4 tsp - ground turmeric
- 1/4 tsp - black pepper
- 1/4 tsp - salt (optional)
- 1 tbsp - lemon juice
- Fresh parsley, chopped (for garnish)

Method
Step 1: Heat the olive oil in a large pot over medium heat. Add the chopped onion and cook until softened, about 5 minutes.
Step 2: Add the minced garlic, diced carrot, and diced celery to the pot. Cook for another 5 minutes, stirring occasionally.
Step 3: Stir in the ground cumin, ground coriander, ground turmeric, and black pepper. Cook for 1 minute until fragrant.
Step 4: Add the rinsed lentils and vegetable broth to the pot. Bring to a boil, then reduce the heat to low and simmer for 20 minutes, or until the lentils are tender.
Step 5: Stir in the chopped spinach and cook for an additional 5 minutes until the spinach is wilted.
Step 6: Add the lemon juice and season with salt if desired. Stir well to combine.
Step 7: Ladle the soup into bowls and garnish with fresh parsley before serving.

Nutritional Values
Cal: 250
Carbs: 35 g
Sugar: 5 g
Protein: 12 g
Fat: 7 g

4.9 Avocado chicken salad

Prep time: 15 min

Cook time: 10 min

Serves: 2

Ingredients

- 1 - Medium avocado, diced
- 1 - Chicken breast, cooked and shredded
- 1 cup - Cherry tomatoes, halved
- 1/4 cup - Red onion, finely chopped
- 1/4 cup - Fresh cilantro, chopped
- 1 - Lime, juiced
- 2 tbsp - Olive oil
- 1/4 tsp - Salt
- 1/4 tsp - Black pepper
- 2 cups - Mixed greens (spinach, arugula, etc.)

Method

Step 1: In a large bowl, combine the diced avocado, shredded chicken, cherry tomatoes, red onion, and fresh cilantro.

Step 2: In a small bowl, whisk together the lime juice, olive oil, salt, and black pepper to make the dressing.

Step 3: Pour the dressing over the salad ingredients and gently toss to combine.

Step 4: Serve the avocado chicken salad over a bed of mixed greens.

Nutritional Values

Cal: 350

Carbs: 12 g

Sugar: 3 g

Protein: 28 g

Fat: 22 g

4.10 Baked salmon with dill yogurt sauce

Prep time: 10 min

Cook time: 20 min

Serves: 2

Ingredients

- 2 fillets - Salmon (about 6 oz each)
- 1 tbsp - Olive oil
- 1/2 tsp - Salt
- 1/4 tsp - Black pepper
- 1 tsp - Lemon zest
- 1 tbsp - Fresh dill, chopped
- 1/2 cup - Plain Greek yogurt
- 1 tbsp - Lemon juice
- 1 clove - Garlic, minced
- 1/4 tsp - Ground cumin
- 1/4 tsp - Paprika

Method

Step 1: Preheat your oven to 375°F (190°C). Line a baking sheet with parchment paper.

Step 2: Rub the salmon fillets with olive oil, and season with salt, black pepper, lemon zest, and paprika. Place the fillets on the prepared baking sheet.

Step 3: Bake the salmon in the preheated oven for 18-20 minutes, or until the fish flakes easily with a fork.

Step 4: While the salmon is baking, prepare the dill yogurt sauce. In a small bowl, combine the Greek yogurt, lemon juice, minced garlic, ground cumin, and chopped dill. Mix well until smooth.

Step 5: Once the salmon is done, remove it from the oven and let it rest for a few minutes.

Step 6: Serve the baked salmon with a generous dollop of dill yogurt sauce on top.

Nutritional Values

Cal: 350

Carbs: 6 g

Sugar: 3 g

Protein: 35 g

Fat: 20 g

4.11 Roasted vegetable quiche

Prep time: 20 min

Cook time: 40 min

Serves: 2

Ingredients

- 1 cup - diced zucchini
- 1 cup - diced bell pepper (red or yellow)
- 1 cup - diced cherry tomatoes
- 1/2 cup - diced red onion
- 1 tbsp - olive oil
- 1/2 tsp - dried thyme
- 1/2 tsp - dried oregano
- 1/4 tsp - salt
- 1/4 tsp - black pepper
- 3 large - eggs
- 1/2 cup - skim milk
- 1/4 cup - grated Parmesan cheese
- 1/4 cup - whole wheat flour
- 1/2 tsp - baking powder
- 1/4 cup - crumbled feta cheese
- 1 tbsp - chopped fresh parsley (optional, for garnish)

Method

Step 1: Preheat your oven to 400°F (200°C). Line a baking sheet with parchment paper.

Step 2: In a large bowl, combine the diced zucchini, bell pepper, cherry tomatoes, and red onion. Drizzle with olive oil, then sprinkle with dried thyme, dried oregano, salt, and black pepper. Toss to coat the vegetables evenly.

Step 3: Spread the seasoned vegetables in a single layer on the prepared baking sheet. Roast in the preheated oven for 20 minutes, or until the vegetables are tender and slightly caramelized. Remove from the oven and set aside.

Step 4: Reduce the oven temperature to 375°F (190°C). Grease a 9-inch pie dish or quiche pan.

Step 5: In a medium bowl, whisk together the eggs, skim milk, and grated Parmesan cheese until well combined.

Step 6: In a separate small bowl, whisk together the whole wheat flour and baking powder. Gradually add the flour mixture to the egg mixture, whisking until smooth.

Step 7: Spread the roasted vegetables evenly in the greased pie dish. Pour the egg mixture over the vegetables, ensuring they are evenly distributed.

Step 8: Sprinkle the crumbled feta cheese on top of the quiche.

Step 9: Bake in the preheated oven for 20 minutes, or until the quiche is set and lightly golden on top.

Step 10: Allow the quiche to cool for a few minutes before slicing. Garnish with chopped fresh parsley, if desired, and serve warm.

Nutritional Values

Cal: 280

Carbs: 20 g

Sugar: 8 g

Protein: 16 g

Fat: 15 g

4.12 Cucumber and hummus sandwiches

Prep time: 10 min

Cook time: 0 min

Serves: 2

Ingredients

- 4 slices - whole grain bread
- 1/2 cup - hummus
- 1 medium - cucumber, thinly sliced
- 1/4 cup - shredded carrots
- 1/4 cup - alfalfa sprouts
- 1/4 tsp - black pepper
- 1/4 tsp - paprika (optional)
- 1 tbsp - olive oil (optional)

Method

Step 1: Spread 2 tablespoons of hummus evenly on each slice of whole grain bread.

Step 2: Layer the cucumber slices evenly on two of the hummus-covered bread slices.

Step 3: Add shredded carrots and alfalfa sprouts on top of the cucumber slices.

Step 4: Sprinkle black pepper and paprika (if using) over the vegetables.

Step 5: Place the remaining hummus-covered bread slices on top to form sandwiches.

Step 6: If desired, lightly brush the outside of the sandwiches with olive oil for added flavor.

Step 7: Cut each sandwich in half and serve immediately.

Nutritional Values

Cal: 250

Carbs: 40 g

Sugar: 5 g

Protein: 8 g

Fat: 8 g

4.13 Spinach and feta stuffed chicken

Prep time: 15 min

Cook time: 25 min

Serves: 2

Ingredients
- 2 - Boneless, skinless chicken breasts
- 1 cup - Fresh spinach, chopped
- 1/2 cup - Feta cheese, crumbled
- 1 clove - Garlic, minced
- 1 tbsp - Olive oil
- 1/2 tsp - Dried oregano
- 1/2 tsp - Dried basil
- Salt and pepper to taste
- 1/2 cup - Low-sodium chicken broth
- 1 tbsp - Lemon juice

Method

Step 1: Preheat the oven to 375°F (190°C).

Step 2: In a small bowl, mix the chopped spinach, feta cheese, minced garlic, dried oregano, and dried basil. Season with a pinch of salt and pepper.

Step 3: Using a sharp knife, carefully cut a pocket into each chicken breast by slicing horizontally but not all the way through.

Step 4: Stuff each chicken breast with the spinach and feta mixture, securing the edges with toothpicks if necessary.

Step 5: Heat the olive oil in an oven-safe skillet over medium-high heat. Sear the stuffed chicken breasts for 2-3 minutes on each side until golden brown.

Step 6: Add the chicken broth and lemon juice to the skillet, then transfer the skillet to the preheated oven.

Step 7: Bake for 20-25 minutes, or until the chicken is cooked through and the internal temperature reaches 165°F (74°C).

Step 8: Remove the chicken from the oven and let it rest for a few minutes before serving.

Nutritional Values

Cal: 320

Carbs: 4 g

Sugar: 1 g

Protein: 42 g

Fat: 15 g

4.14 Asian beef salad

Prep time: 20 min
Cook time: 10 min
Serves: 2

Ingredients
- 200g - lean beef sirloin, thinly sliced
- 1 tbsp - low-sodium soy sauce
- 1 tbsp - lime juice
- 1 tsp - sesame oil
- 1 clove - garlic, minced
- 1 tsp - fresh ginger, grated
- 1/2 - red bell pepper, thinly sliced
- 1/2 - yellow bell pepper, thinly sliced
- 1/2 - cucumber, thinly sliced
- 1 - carrot, julienned
- 2 cups - mixed salad greens
- 1/4 cup - fresh cilantro, chopped
- 1/4 cup - fresh mint, chopped
- 1 tbsp - sesame seeds, toasted
- 1 tbsp - olive oil
- 1 tbsp - rice vinegar
- 1 tsp - honey
- Salt and pepper to taste

Method
Step 1: In a bowl, combine the soy sauce, lime juice, sesame oil, garlic, and ginger. Add the beef slices and marinate for 10 minutes.
Step 2: Heat a non-stick skillet over medium-high heat. Add the marinated beef and cook for 2-3 minutes on each side until browned and cooked through. Remove from heat and set aside.
Step 3: In a large bowl, combine the red bell pepper, yellow bell pepper, cucumber, carrot, mixed salad greens, cilantro, and mint.
Step 4: In a small bowl, whisk together the olive oil, rice vinegar, honey, salt, and pepper to make the dressing.
Step 5: Add the cooked beef to the salad and drizzle with the dressing. Toss gently to combine.
Step 6: Sprinkle with toasted sesame seeds before serving.

Nutritional Values
Cal: 350
Carbs: 20 g
Sugar: 8 g
Protein: 30 g
Fat: 15 g

4.15 Shrimp and avocado taco salad

Prep time: 15 min
Cook time: 10 min
Serves: 2

Ingredients
- 200g - Shrimp, peeled and deveined
- 1 - Avocado, diced
- 1 cup - Cherry tomatoes, halved
- 1/2 cup - Red onion, finely chopped
- 2 cups - Romaine lettuce, chopped
- 1/4 cup - Fresh cilantro, chopped
- 1 - Lime, juiced
- 1 tbsp - Olive oil
- 1 tsp - Cumin
- 1 tsp - Paprika
- 1/2 tsp - Garlic powder
- Salt and pepper to taste
- 1 - Jalapeño, sliced (optional)

Method
Step 1: In a small bowl, mix together the cumin, paprika, garlic powder, salt, and pepper. Sprinkle this spice mixture over the shrimp, ensuring they are evenly coated.
Step 2: Heat the olive oil in a skillet over medium heat. Add the shrimp and cook for 2-3 minutes on each side, or until they are pink and opaque. Remove from heat and set aside.
Step 3: In a large salad bowl, combine the chopped romaine lettuce, cherry tomatoes, red onion, and cilantro.
Step 4: Add the cooked shrimp and diced avocado to the salad bowl.
Step 5: Drizzle the lime juice over the salad and toss gently to combine all ingredients.
Step 6: Garnish with sliced jalapeño if desired and serve immediately.

Nutritional Values
Cal: 350
Carbs: 20 g
Sugar: 5 g
Protein: 25 g
Fat: 20 g

4.16 Butternut squash and chickpea curry

Prep time: 15 min

Cook time: 30 min

Serves: 2

Ingredients
- 1 cup - Butternut squash, peeled and cubed
- 1/2 cup - Canned chickpeas, drained and rinsed
- 1/2 - Medium onion, finely chopped
- 1 - Garlic clove, minced
- 1/2 inch - Fresh ginger, grated
- 1 - Medium tomato, chopped
- 1/2 cup - Light coconut milk
- 1/2 cup - Vegetable broth
- 1 tbsp - Olive oil
- 1 tsp - Ground cumin
- 1 tsp - Ground coriander
- 1/2 tsp - Ground turmeric
- 1/4 tsp - Ground cinnamon
- 1/4 tsp - Red chili flakes (optional)
- 1/4 tsp - Salt
- 1/4 tsp - Black pepper
- 1 tbsp - Fresh cilantro, chopped (for garnish)
- 1/2 - Lime, juiced

Method

Step 1: Heat the olive oil in a large pan over medium heat. Add the chopped onion and sauté until translucent, about 5 minutes.

Step 2: Add the minced garlic and grated ginger to the pan, and sauté for another 2 minutes until fragrant.

Step 3: Stir in the ground cumin, ground coriander, ground turmeric, ground cinnamon, and red chili flakes (if using). Cook for 1 minute to toast the spices.

Step 4: Add the chopped tomato to the pan and cook until it starts to break down, about 3 minutes.

Step 5: Add the cubed butternut squash, drained chickpeas, vegetable broth, and coconut milk to the pan. Stir to combine.

Step 6: Bring the mixture to a boil, then reduce the heat to low and simmer for 20 minutes, or until the butternut squash is tender.

Step 7: Season with salt and black pepper to taste. Stir in the lime juice.

Step 8: Garnish with fresh cilantro before serving.

Nutritional Values

Cal: 350

Carbs: 45 g

Sugar: 8 g

Protein: 10 g

Fat: 14 g

4.17 Pear and walnut salad

Prep time: 15 min

Cook time: 0 min

Serves: 2

Ingredients

- 2 cups - Mixed salad greens (spinach, arugula, and lettuce)
- 1 - Ripe pear, thinly sliced
- 1/4 cup - Walnuts, toasted and roughly chopped
- 1/4 cup - Crumbled feta cheese
- 1/4 cup - Dried cranberries (unsweetened)
- 1/2 - Small red onion, thinly sliced
- 2 tbsp - Extra virgin olive oil
- 1 tbsp - Balsamic vinegar
- 1 tsp - Dijon mustard
- Salt and pepper to taste

Method

Step 1: In a large bowl, combine the mixed salad greens, sliced pear, walnuts, feta cheese, dried cranberries, and red onion.

Step 2: In a small bowl, whisk together the olive oil, balsamic vinegar, Dijon mustard, salt, and pepper until well combined.

Step 3: Drizzle the dressing over the salad and toss gently to combine.

Step 4: Divide the salad into two serving bowls and serve immediately.

Nutritional Values

Cal: 320

Carbs: 28 g

Sugar: 16 g

Protein: 7 g

Fat: 22 g

4.18 Turkey meatball soup

Prep time: 15 min
Cook time: 30 min
Serves: 2

Ingredients
- 200g - Ground turkey
- 1 - Egg
- 2 tbsp - Whole wheat breadcrumbs
- 1 clove - Garlic, minced
- 1/4 cup - Onion, finely chopped
- 1/4 tsp - Dried oregano
- 1/4 tsp - Dried basil
- 1/4 tsp - Salt
- 1/4 tsp - Black pepper
- 1 tbsp - Olive oil
- 4 cups - Low-sodium chicken broth
- 1 - Carrot, sliced
- 1 - Celery stalk, sliced
- 1/2 cup - Zucchini, diced
- 1/2 cup - Spinach, chopped
- 1/4 cup - Fresh parsley, chopped

Method
Step 1: In a large bowl, combine the ground turkey, egg, whole wheat breadcrumbs, minced garlic, chopped onion, dried oregano, dried basil, salt, and black pepper. Mix well until all ingredients are evenly incorporated.
Step 2: Form the mixture into small meatballs, about 1 inch in diameter.
Step 3: Heat the olive oil in a large pot over medium heat. Add the meatballs and cook until browned on all sides, about 5-7 minutes. Remove the meatballs from the pot and set aside.
Step 4: In the same pot, add the low-sodium chicken broth, sliced carrot, and sliced celery. Bring to a boil, then reduce the heat and let it simmer for 10 minutes.
Step 5: Add the diced zucchini and chopped spinach to the pot. Return the meatballs to the pot and let everything simmer for another 10 minutes, or until the vegetables are tender and the meatballs are cooked through.
Step 6: Stir in the fresh parsley and adjust seasoning with additional salt and pepper if needed. Serve hot.

Nutritional Values
Cal: 350
Carbs: 18 g
Sugar: 6 g
Protein: 35 g
Fat: 15 g

4.19 Eggplant and mozzarella bake

Prep time: 15 min

Cook time: 35 min

Serves: 2

Ingredients
- 1 medium eggplant, sliced into 1/4-inch rounds
- 1 cup marinara sauce (low-sodium)
- 1 cup shredded mozzarella cheese (part-skim)
- 1/4 cup grated Parmesan cheese
- 1/4 cup fresh basil leaves, chopped
- 1 tbsp olive oil
- 1/2 tsp dried oregano
- 1/4 tsp black pepper
- 1/4 tsp salt

Method

Step 1: Preheat your oven to 375°F (190°C). Lightly grease a baking dish with olive oil.

Step 2: Arrange the eggplant slices in a single layer on a baking sheet. Brush both sides with olive oil and sprinkle with salt and black pepper. Bake for 15 minutes, turning halfway through, until tender and lightly browned.

Step 3: In the greased baking dish, spread a thin layer of marinara sauce. Place a layer of baked eggplant slices over the sauce.

Step 4: Sprinkle a portion of the mozzarella cheese over the eggplant, followed by a sprinkle of Parmesan cheese and some chopped basil.

Step 5: Repeat the layers until all ingredients are used, finishing with a layer of cheese on top. Sprinkle the dried oregano over the final layer.

Step 6: Bake in the preheated oven for 20 minutes, or until the cheese is melted and bubbly. Let it cool for a few minutes before serving.

Nutritional Values

Cal: 320

Carbs: 20 g

Sugar: 10 g

Protein: 18 g

Fat: 20 g

4.20 Cold beet and yogurt soup

Prep time: 15 min

Cook time: 0 min

Serves: 2

Ingredients

- 2 medium beets, cooked and peeled
- 1 cup plain Greek yogurt
- 1/2 cup cold water
- 1 small cucumber, peeled and diced
- 1 garlic clove, minced
- 1 tablespoon fresh dill, chopped
- 1 tablespoon fresh lemon juice
- Salt and pepper to taste
- 1 tablespoon olive oil (optional for garnish)
- 2 tablespoons crumbled feta cheese (optional for garnish)

Method

Step 1: Grate the cooked and peeled beets using a box grater or food processor.

Step 2: In a large bowl, combine the grated beets, Greek yogurt, and cold water. Mix well until smooth.

Step 3: Add the diced cucumber, minced garlic, chopped dill, and fresh lemon juice to the bowl. Stir to combine.

Step 4: Season with salt and pepper to taste. Adjust the consistency with additional water if needed.

Step 5: Chill the soup in the refrigerator for at least 30 minutes before serving.

Step 6: Serve the cold beet and yogurt soup in bowls. Drizzle with olive oil and sprinkle with crumbled feta cheese if desired.

Nutritional Values

Cal: 150

Carbs: 18 g

Sugar: 12 g

Protein: 8 g

Fat: 5 g

5. Satisfying dinner recipes
5.1 Grilled salmon with dill yogurt sauce

Prep time: 15 min

Cook time: 10 min

Serves: 2

Ingredients
- 2 fillets - Salmon (about 6 oz each)
- 1 tbsp - Olive oil
- 1/2 tsp - Salt
- 1/4 tsp - Black pepper
- 1/2 cup - Greek yogurt
- 1 tbsp - Fresh dill, chopped
- 1 tbsp - Lemon juice
- 1 clove - Garlic, minced
- 1/2 tsp - Lemon zest
- 1/4 tsp - Ground black pepper
- 1/4 tsp - Salt
- 1/2 - Cucumber, finely diced

Method

Step 1: Preheat your grill to medium-high heat. Brush the salmon fillets with olive oil and season with salt and black pepper.

Step 2: Place the salmon fillets on the grill, skin-side down. Grill for about 4-5 minutes on each side, or until the salmon is cooked through and flakes easily with a fork.

Step 3: While the salmon is grilling, prepare the dill yogurt sauce. In a small bowl, combine the Greek yogurt, fresh dill, lemon juice, minced garlic, lemon zest, ground black pepper, salt, and finely diced cucumber. Mix well.

Step 4: Once the salmon is done, remove it from the grill and let it rest for a couple of minutes.

Step 5: Serve the grilled salmon fillets with a generous dollop of dill yogurt sauce on top. Enjoy your healthy and satisfying dinner!

Nutritional Values

Cal: 350

Carbs: 8 g

Sugar: 4 g

Protein: 35 g

Fat: 20 g

5.2 Chicken and vegetable stir-fry

Prep time: 15 min
Cook time: 10 min
Serves: 2

Ingredients
- 200g - Chicken breast, thinly sliced
- 1 tbsp - Olive oil
- 1 - Red bell pepper, thinly sliced
- 1 - Yellow bell pepper, thinly sliced
- 1 - Medium carrot, julienned
- 1 cup - Broccoli florets
- 2 cloves - Garlic, minced
- 1 tbsp - Fresh ginger, minced
- 2 tbsp - Low-sodium soy sauce
- 1 tbsp - Oyster sauce
- 1 tsp - Sesame oil
- 1 tsp - Cornstarch mixed with 2 tbsp water
- 2 - Green onions, sliced
- 1 tbsp - Sesame seeds (optional)

Method
Step 1: Heat the olive oil in a large skillet or wok over medium-high heat. Add the chicken slices and stir-fry until cooked through, about 5-7 minutes. Remove the chicken from the skillet and set aside.
Step 2: In the same skillet, add the garlic and ginger, and stir-fry for about 30 seconds until fragrant.
Step 3: Add the red and yellow bell peppers, carrot, and broccoli to the skillet. Stir-fry for about 3-4 minutes until the vegetables are tender-crisp.
Step 4: Return the cooked chicken to the skillet. Add the soy sauce, oyster sauce, and sesame oil. Stir well to combine.
Step 5: Pour the cornstarch mixture into the skillet and stir continuously until the sauce thickens, about 1-2 minutes.
Step 6: Garnish with sliced green onions and sesame seeds, if using. Serve hot.

Nutritional Values
Cal: 350
Carbs: 20 g
Sugar: 6 g
Protein: 35 g
Fat: 15 g

5.3 Lentil soup with kale

Prep time: 15 min
Cook time: 30 min
Serves: 2

Ingredients
- 1 tablespoon - olive oil
- 1 small - onion, finely chopped
- 2 cloves - garlic, minced
- 1 medium - carrot, diced
- 1 stalk - celery, diced
- 1/2 cup - dried green or brown lentils, rinsed
- 4 cups - low-sodium vegetable broth
- 1/2 teaspoon - ground cumin
- 1/2 teaspoon - ground coriander
- 1/4 teaspoon - smoked paprika
- 1/4 teaspoon - black pepper
- 2 cups - chopped kale, stems removed
- 1 tablespoon - lemon juice
- Salt to taste

Method
Step 1: Heat the olive oil in a large pot over medium heat. Add the chopped onion and sauté for about 5 minutes, until translucent.
Step 2: Add the minced garlic, diced carrot, and diced celery to the pot. Cook for another 5 minutes, stirring occasionally.
Step 3: Add the rinsed lentils, vegetable broth, ground cumin, ground coriander, smoked paprika, and black pepper to the pot. Bring to a boil, then reduce the heat and let it simmer for 20 minutes, or until the lentils are tender.
Step 4: Stir in the chopped kale and cook for an additional 5 minutes, until the kale is wilted.
Step 5: Add the lemon juice and salt to taste. Stir well and serve hot.

Nutritional Values
Cal: 250
Carbs: 35 g
Sugar: 6 g
Protein: 12 g
Fat: 7 g

5.4 Zucchini noodles with pesto

Prep time: 15 min

Cook time: 10 min

Serves: 2

Ingredients

- 2 medium zucchinis - Zucchini
- 1 cup - Fresh basil leaves
- 1/4 cup - Pine nuts
- 1/4 cup - Grated Parmesan cheese
- 1 clove - Garlic
- 1/4 cup - Extra virgin olive oil
- 1 tbsp - Lemon juice
- Salt and pepper to taste
- 1/2 cup - Cherry tomatoes (halved)
- 1 tbsp - Olive oil (for cooking zucchini noodles)

Method

Step 1: Wash and trim the ends of the zucchinis. Use a spiralizer to create zucchini noodles (zoodles). Set aside.

Step 2: In a food processor, combine the basil leaves, pine nuts, Parmesan cheese, and garlic. Pulse until finely chopped.

Step 3: With the food processor running, slowly add the extra virgin olive oil and lemon juice until the mixture is smooth. Season with salt and pepper to taste.

Step 4: Heat 1 tbsp of olive oil in a large skillet over medium heat. Add the zucchini noodles and sauté for 2-3 minutes until just tender.

Step 5: Remove the skillet from heat and toss the zucchini noodles with the prepared pesto sauce until well coated.

Step 6: Serve the zucchini noodles topped with halved cherry tomatoes.

Nutritional Values

Cal: 350

Carbs: 10 g

Sugar: 5 g

Protein: 8 g

Fat: 30 g

5.5 Baked tilapia with lemon and herbs

Prep time: 10 min

Cook time: 20 min

Serves: 2

Ingredients
- 2 fillets - Tilapia
- 1 - Lemon (sliced)
- 2 tbsp - Olive oil
- 1 tsp - Dried thyme
- 1 tsp - Dried rosemary
- 1 tsp - Dried parsley
- 2 cloves - Garlic (minced)
- 1/2 tsp - Salt
- 1/4 tsp - Black pepper
- 1/2 cup - Cherry tomatoes (halved)
- 1/2 - Red onion (sliced)
- 1/4 cup - Fresh parsley (chopped, for garnish)

Method

Step 1: Preheat the oven to 375°F (190°C).

Step 2: Place the tilapia fillets on a baking sheet lined with parchment paper.

Step 3: Drizzle the olive oil over the tilapia fillets.

Step 4: In a small bowl, mix together the dried thyme, dried rosemary, dried parsley, minced garlic, salt, and black pepper.

Step 5: Sprinkle the herb mixture evenly over the tilapia fillets.

Step 6: Arrange the lemon slices, cherry tomatoes, and red onion slices around the tilapia fillets on the baking sheet.

Step 7: Bake in the preheated oven for 20 minutes, or until the tilapia is cooked through and flakes easily with a fork.

Step 8: Remove from the oven and garnish with fresh parsley before serving.

Nutritional Values

Cal: 320

Carbs: 8 g

Sugar: 4 g

Protein: 35 g

Fat: 18 g

5.6 Vegetarian chili

Prep time: 15 min

Cook time: 30 min

Serves: 2

Ingredients

- 1 tbsp - Olive oil
- 1 - Small onion, diced
- 1 - Red bell pepper, diced
- 2 cloves - Garlic, minced
- 1 - Jalapeño, seeded and minced
- 1 tsp - Ground cumin
- 1 tsp - Chili powder
- 1/2 tsp - Smoked paprika
- 1/2 tsp - Ground coriander
- 1 can (15 oz) - Black beans, drained and rinsed
- 1 can (15 oz) - Kidney beans, drained and rinsed
- 1 can (14.5 oz) - Diced tomatoes
- 1 cup - Vegetable broth
- 1/2 tsp - Salt
- 1/4 tsp - Black pepper
- 1/2 cup - Corn kernels (fresh or frozen)
- 1/4 cup - Chopped fresh cilantro
- 1 - Avocado, sliced (for garnish)
- 2 tbsp - Sour cream (optional, for garnish)
- 1 - Lime, cut into wedges (for garnish)

Method

Step 1: Heat the olive oil in a large pot over medium heat. Add the diced onion and red bell pepper, and sauté for about 5 minutes until softened.

Step 2: Add the minced garlic and jalapeño to the pot and cook for another 1-2 minutes until fragrant.

Step 3: Stir in the ground cumin, chili powder, smoked paprika, and ground coriander, and cook for 1 minute to toast the spices.

Step 4: Add the black beans, kidney beans, diced tomatoes, vegetable broth, salt, and black pepper to the pot. Stir to combine and bring to a simmer.

Step 5: Reduce the heat to low and let the chili simmer for 20 minutes, stirring occasionally.

Step 6: Stir in the corn kernels and cook for an additional 5 minutes.

Step 7: Remove the pot from heat and stir in the chopped fresh cilantro.

Step 8: Serve the chili in bowls, garnished with sliced avocado, a dollop of sour cream (if using), and lime wedges on the side.

Nutritional Values

Cal: 350

Carbs: 55 g

Sugar: 8 g

Protein: 14 g

Fat: 10 g

5.7 Grilled chicken caesar salad

Prep time: 15 min
Cook time: 10 min
Serves: 2

Ingredients
- 2 - Boneless, skinless chicken breasts
- 1 tbsp - Olive oil
- 1 tsp - Garlic powder
- 1 tsp - Onion powder
- 1 tsp - Dried oregano
- 1 tsp - Dried basil
- 1/2 tsp - Salt
- 1/2 tsp - Black pepper
- 4 cups - Romaine lettuce, chopped
- 1/4 cup - Grated Parmesan cheese
- 1/2 cup - Cherry tomatoes, halved
- 1/4 cup - Caesar dressing (low-fat or diabetic-friendly)
- 1/2 cup - Whole grain croutons (optional)

Method
Step 1: Preheat the grill to medium-high heat.
Step 2: In a small bowl, mix together the olive oil, garlic powder, onion powder, dried oregano, dried basil, salt, and black pepper.
Step 3: Brush the chicken breasts with the olive oil mixture, ensuring they are evenly coated.
Step 4: Place the chicken breasts on the grill and cook for 5-7 minutes on each side, or until the internal temperature reaches 165°F (74°C).
Step 5: Remove the chicken from the grill and let it rest for 5 minutes before slicing it into thin strips.
Step 6: In a large salad bowl, combine the chopped romaine lettuce, grated Parmesan cheese, and cherry tomatoes.
Step 7: Add the sliced grilled chicken to the salad.
Step 8: Drizzle the Caesar dressing over the salad and toss to combine.
Step 9: Top with whole grain croutons if desired.

Nutritional Values
Cal: 350
Carbs: 12 g
Sugar: 4 g
Protein: 40 g
Fat: 18 g

5.8 Beef and broccoli

Prep time: 15 min
Cook time: 20 min
Serves: 2

Ingredients
- 200g - Beef sirloin, thinly sliced
- 1 cup - Broccoli florets
- 1/2 - Red bell pepper, sliced
- 1/2 - Onion, sliced
- 2 cloves - Garlic, minced
- 1 tbsp - Olive oil
- 2 tbsp - Low-sodium soy sauce
- 1 tbsp - Oyster sauce
- 1 tsp - Cornstarch
- 1/4 cup - Water
- 1/2 tsp - Fresh ginger, grated
- 1/2 tsp - Sesame oil
- 1/2 tsp - Black pepper
- 1/4 tsp - Red pepper flakes (optional)

Method
Step 1: In a small bowl, mix the soy sauce, oyster sauce, cornstarch, and water until smooth. Set aside.
Step 2: Heat the olive oil in a large skillet over medium-high heat. Add the garlic and ginger, and sauté for 1 minute until fragrant.
Step 3: Add the beef slices to the skillet and cook for 3-4 minutes, until browned. Remove the beef from the skillet and set aside.
Step 4: In the same skillet, add the broccoli, red bell pepper, and onion. Stir-fry for 5-6 minutes until the vegetables are tender-crisp.
Step 5: Return the beef to the skillet and pour in the sauce mixture. Stir well to combine and cook for another 2-3 minutes until the sauce thickens.
Step 6: Drizzle with sesame oil, sprinkle with black pepper and red pepper flakes (if using), and serve hot.

Nutritional Values
Cal: 350
Carbs: 15 g
Sugar: 5 g
Protein: 30 g
Fat: 18 g

5.9 Spaghetti squash with marinara sauce

Prep time: 15 min
Cook time: 40 min
Serves: 2

Ingredients
- 1 medium spaghetti squash
- 1 cup marinara sauce (low-sugar)
- 1 tablespoon olive oil
- 1/2 teaspoon salt
- 1/4 teaspoon black pepper
- 1/2 teaspoon dried oregano
- 1/2 teaspoon dried basil
- 1/4 cup grated Parmesan cheese
- 2 tablespoons chopped fresh parsley (optional)

Method
Step 1: Preheat your oven to 400°F (200°C). Line a baking sheet with parchment paper.
Step 2: Cut the spaghetti squash in half lengthwise and scoop out the seeds.
Step 3: Drizzle the inside of each squash half with olive oil and season with salt and black pepper.
Step 4: Place the squash halves cut-side down on the prepared baking sheet. Bake for 35-40 minutes, or until the flesh is tender and easily pierced with a fork.
Step 5: While the squash is baking, heat the marinara sauce in a small saucepan over medium heat. Stir in the dried oregano and dried basil. Simmer for 5-10 minutes, then remove from heat.
Step 6: Once the squash is done, remove it from the oven and let it cool slightly. Use a fork to scrape the flesh into spaghetti-like strands.
Step 7: Divide the spaghetti squash strands between two plates. Top each serving with half of the marinara sauce.
Step 8: Sprinkle each serving with grated Parmesan cheese and garnish with chopped fresh parsley if desired.

Nutritional Values
Cal: 210
Carbs: 25 g
Sugar: 10 g
Protein: 6 g
Fat: 10 g

5.10 Pork tenderloin with apple cider glaze

Prep time: 15 min
Cook time: 25 min
Serves: 2

Ingredients
- 1 - Pork tenderloin (about 12 oz)
- 1/2 cup - Apple cider
- 1 tbsp - Olive oil
- 1 tbsp - Dijon mustard
- 1 tbsp - Apple cider vinegar
- 1 tbsp - Honey
- 1 clove - Garlic, minced
- 1/2 tsp - Fresh thyme, chopped
- 1/4 tsp - Salt
- 1/4 tsp - Black pepper
- 1 - Granny Smith apple, thinly sliced
- 1/2 - Red onion, thinly sliced

Method
Step 1: Preheat the oven to 375°F (190°C). Season the pork tenderloin with salt and black pepper.
Step 2: In a large oven-safe skillet, heat the olive oil over medium-high heat. Sear the pork tenderloin on all sides until browned, about 2-3 minutes per side.
Step 3: In a small bowl, whisk together the apple cider, Dijon mustard, apple cider vinegar, honey, garlic, and fresh thyme.
Step 4: Pour the apple cider mixture over the pork tenderloin in the skillet. Add the sliced apple and red onion around the pork.
Step 5: Transfer the skillet to the preheated oven and roast for 15-20 minutes, or until the internal temperature of the pork reaches 145°F (63°C).
Step 6: Remove the skillet from the oven and let the pork rest for 5 minutes before slicing. Serve with the apple and onion mixture, drizzling some of the glaze over the top.

Nutritional Values
Cal: 350
Carbs: 25 g
Sugar: 18 g
Protein: 30 g
Fat: 12 g

5.11 Shrimp and asparagus stir-fry

Prep time: 15 min
Cook time: 10 min
Serves: 2

Ingredients
- 200g - Shrimp, peeled and deveined
- 200g - Asparagus, trimmed and cut into 2-inch pieces
- 1 - Red bell pepper, thinly sliced
- 2 - Garlic cloves, minced
- 1 tbsp - Fresh ginger, grated
- 2 tbsp - Low-sodium soy sauce
- 1 tbsp - Oyster sauce
- 1 tbsp - Olive oil
- 1 tsp - Sesame oil
- 1/4 tsp - Red pepper flakes (optional)
- 1 tbsp - Sesame seeds (optional)
- 2 - Green onions, chopped
- Salt and pepper to taste

Method
Step 1: Heat the olive oil in a large skillet or wok over medium-high heat. Add the garlic and ginger, and sauté for 1 minute until fragrant.
Step 2: Add the shrimp to the skillet and cook for 2-3 minutes until they start to turn pink. Remove the shrimp from the skillet and set aside.
Step 3: In the same skillet, add the asparagus and red bell pepper. Stir-fry for 3-4 minutes until the vegetables are tender-crisp.
Step 4: Return the shrimp to the skillet. Add the soy sauce, oyster sauce, and sesame oil. Stir well to combine all the ingredients.
Step 5: Cook for an additional 2-3 minutes until the shrimp are fully cooked and the sauce has thickened slightly.
Step 6: Season with red pepper flakes, salt, and pepper to taste. Garnish with sesame seeds and chopped green onions before serving.

Nutritional Values
Cal: 250
Carbs: 12 g
Sugar: 5 g
Protein: 30 g
Fat: 10 g

5.12 Eggplant parmesan

Prep time: 20 min

Cook time: 30 min

Serves: 2

Ingredients

- 1 medium eggplant
- 1/2 cup - whole wheat breadcrumbs
- 1/4 cup - grated Parmesan cheese
- 1/2 cup - shredded part-skim mozzarella cheese
- 1 large egg
- 1/2 cup - unsweetened almond milk
- 1 cup - marinara sauce (low-sodium)
- 1 tablespoon - olive oil
- 1 teaspoon - dried oregano
- 1 teaspoon - dried basil
- 1/2 teaspoon - garlic powder
- Salt and pepper to taste
- Fresh basil leaves for garnish (optional)

Method

Step 1: Preheat your oven to 375°F (190°C). Line a baking sheet with parchment paper.

Step 2: Slice the eggplant into 1/4-inch thick rounds. Sprinkle both sides lightly with salt and let sit for 10 minutes to draw out moisture. Pat dry with paper towels.

Step 3: In a shallow bowl, combine the whole wheat breadcrumbs, grated Parmesan cheese, dried oregano, dried basil, garlic powder, salt, and pepper.

Step 4: In another shallow bowl, whisk together the egg and unsweetened almond milk.

Step 5: Dip each eggplant slice into the egg mixture, then coat with the breadcrumb mixture, pressing gently to adhere.

Step 6: Heat olive oil in a large skillet over medium heat. Fry the eggplant slices until golden brown on both sides, about 2-3 minutes per side. Transfer to the prepared baking sheet.

Step 7: Spread a thin layer of marinara sauce on the bottom of a small baking dish. Arrange half of the eggplant slices in a single layer over the sauce.

Step 8: Spoon half of the remaining marinara sauce over the eggplant, then sprinkle with half of the shredded mozzarella cheese.

Step 9: Repeat with the remaining eggplant slices, marinara sauce, and mozzarella cheese.

Step 10: Bake in the preheated oven for 20 minutes, or until the cheese is melted and bubbly.

Step 11: Let cool for a few minutes before serving. Garnish with fresh basil leaves if desired.

Nutritional Values

Cal: 320

Carbs: 30 g

Sugar: 8 g

Protein: 18 g

Fat: 15 g

5.13 Cauliflower rice pilaf

Prep time: 15 min
Cook time: 15 min
Serves: 2

Ingredients
- 1 medium head - Cauliflower
- 1 tbsp - Olive oil
- 1 small - Onion, finely chopped
- 1 clove - Garlic, minced
- 1/2 cup - Carrots, diced
- 1/2 cup - Peas (fresh or frozen)
- 1/4 cup - Slivered almonds, toasted
- 1/4 cup - Fresh parsley, chopped
- 1/2 tsp - Ground cumin
- 1/4 tsp - Ground turmeric
- Salt and pepper to taste
- 1/2 lemon - Juice

Method
Step 1: Cut the cauliflower into florets and pulse in a food processor until it resembles rice.
Step 2: Heat the olive oil in a large skillet over medium heat. Add the onion and cook until translucent, about 3-4 minutes.
Step 3: Add the garlic and cook for another minute until fragrant.
Step 4: Stir in the carrots and cook for 5 minutes until they begin to soften.
Step 5: Add the cauliflower rice, peas, cumin, turmeric, salt, and pepper. Cook for 5-7 minutes, stirring occasionally, until the cauliflower is tender.
Step 6: Remove from heat and stir in the toasted almonds, fresh parsley, and lemon juice.
Step 7: Serve warm.

Nutritional Values
Cal: 210
Carbs: 20 g
Sugar: 6 g
Protein: 6 g
Fat: 12 g

5.14 Balsamic glazed salmon

Prep time: 10 min

Cook time: 15 min

Serves: 2

Ingredients

- 2 - Salmon fillets (about 6 oz each)
- 1/4 cup - Balsamic vinegar
- 2 tbsp - Honey
- 1 tbsp - Dijon mustard
- 2 cloves - Garlic, minced
- 1 tbsp - Olive oil
- 1/2 tsp - Salt
- 1/4 tsp - Black pepper
- 1 tbsp - Fresh parsley, chopped (for garnish)

Method

Step 1: Preheat the oven to 400°F (200°C). Line a baking sheet with parchment paper or lightly grease it with olive oil.

Step 2: In a small bowl, whisk together the balsamic vinegar, honey, Dijon mustard, and minced garlic until well combined.

Step 3: Place the salmon fillets on the prepared baking sheet. Brush the balsamic mixture generously over the salmon fillets, coating them evenly.

Step 4: Season the salmon fillets with salt and black pepper.

Step 5: Bake the salmon in the preheated oven for 12-15 minutes, or until the salmon is cooked through and flakes easily with a fork.

Step 6: Remove the salmon from the oven and let it rest for a few minutes. Garnish with chopped fresh parsley before serving.

Nutritional Values

Cal: 350

Carbs: 20 g

Sugar: 15 g

Protein: 30 g

Fat: 15 g

5.15 Chickpea and spinach curry

Prep time: 15 min

Cook time: 25 min

Serves: 2

Ingredients

- 1 tbsp - Olive oil
- 1 small - Onion, finely chopped
- 2 cloves - Garlic, minced
- 1 inch - Ginger, grated
- 1 tsp - Ground cumin
- 1 tsp - Ground coriander
- 1/2 tsp - Turmeric powder
- 1/2 tsp - Garam masala
- 1/4 tsp - Red chili powder (optional)
- 1 can (400g) - Chickpeas, drained and rinsed
- 2 cups - Fresh spinach, chopped
- 1 can (400g) - Diced tomatoes
- 1/2 cup - Coconut milk
- Salt to taste
- Fresh cilantro, chopped (for garnish)

Method

Step 1: Heat the olive oil in a large pan over medium heat. Add the finely chopped onion and sauté until it becomes translucent, about 5 minutes.

Step 2: Add the minced garlic and grated ginger to the pan, and sauté for another 2 minutes until fragrant.

Step 3: Stir in the ground cumin, ground coriander, turmeric powder, garam masala, and red chili powder (if using). Cook for 1 minute to toast the spices.

Step 4: Add the drained and rinsed chickpeas to the pan, stirring to coat them with the spices.

Step 5: Pour in the diced tomatoes and coconut milk, and bring the mixture to a simmer. Cook for 10 minutes, allowing the flavors to meld together.

Step 6: Add the chopped spinach to the pan, stirring until it wilts and is well incorporated into the curry, about 3 minutes.

Step 7: Season the curry with salt to taste. Simmer for an additional 2 minutes to ensure everything is heated through.

Step 8: Serve the chickpea and spinach curry hot, garnished with fresh chopped cilantro.

Nutritional Values

Cal: 350

Carbs: 45 g

Sugar: 8 g

Protein: 12 g

Fat: 15 g

5.16 Stuffed acorn squash

Prep time: 15 min

Cook time: 45 min

Serves: 2

Ingredients

- 1 medium - Acorn squash
- 1/2 cup - Quinoa
- 1 cup - Vegetable broth
- 1/2 medium - Onion, finely chopped
- 1 clove - Garlic, minced
- 1/2 cup - Baby spinach, chopped
- 1/4 cup - Dried cranberries
- 1/4 cup - Pecans, chopped
- 1 tbsp - Olive oil
- 1/2 tsp - Dried thyme
- 1/2 tsp - Dried sage
- Salt and pepper to taste

Method

Step 1: Preheat the oven to 400°F (200°C). Cut the acorn squash in half lengthwise and scoop out the seeds. Brush the inside of each half with olive oil and season with salt and pepper. Place the squash halves cut side down on a baking sheet and roast for 30-35 minutes, or until tender.

Step 2: While the squash is roasting, rinse the quinoa under cold water. In a medium saucepan, bring the vegetable broth to a boil. Add the quinoa, reduce the heat to low, cover, and simmer for about 15 minutes, or until the quinoa is cooked and the liquid is absorbed. Fluff with a fork and set aside.

Step 3: In a skillet, heat the remaining olive oil over medium heat. Add the chopped onion and cook until translucent, about 5 minutes. Add the minced garlic and cook for another 1-2 minutes. Stir in the chopped spinach, dried cranberries, and chopped pecans. Cook until the spinach is wilted.

Step 4: Add the cooked quinoa to the skillet and stir to combine. Season with dried thyme, dried sage, salt, and pepper. Mix well and cook for another 2-3 minutes to allow the flavors to meld.

Step 5: Remove the roasted squash from the oven and carefully turn them over. Fill each squash half with the quinoa mixture, pressing down lightly to pack the filling. Return the stuffed squash to the oven and bake for an additional 10 minutes.

Step 6: Serve the stuffed acorn squash hot, garnished with additional chopped pecans if desired.

Nutritional Values

Cal: 350

Carbs: 55 g

Sugar: 12 g

Protein: 8 g

Fat: 12 g

5.17 Quinoa and black bean stuffed peppers

Prep time: 20 min

Cook time: 30 min

Serves: 2

Ingredients
- 2 large bell peppers (any color)
- 1/2 cup quinoa
- 1 cup water
- 1/2 cup black beans, drained and rinsed
- 1/2 cup corn kernels (fresh, frozen, or canned)
- 1/4 cup diced tomatoes
- 1/4 cup diced red onion
- 1 clove garlic, minced
- 1/2 tsp cumin
- 1/2 tsp chili powder
- 1/4 tsp salt
- 1/4 tsp black pepper
- 1/4 cup shredded low-fat cheddar cheese
- 1 tbsp chopped fresh cilantro (optional)
- 1 tbsp olive oil

Method
Step 1: Preheat the oven to 375°F (190°C). Cut the tops off the bell peppers and remove the seeds and membranes. Set aside.
Step 2: In a medium saucepan, bring the water to a boil. Add the quinoa, reduce heat to low, cover, and simmer for about 15 minutes, or until the water is absorbed and the quinoa is tender.
Step 3: In a large skillet, heat the olive oil over medium heat. Add the red onion and garlic, and sauté until softened, about 3-4 minutes.
Step 4: Add the cooked quinoa, black beans, corn, diced tomatoes, cumin, chili powder, salt, and black pepper to the skillet. Stir to combine and cook for another 5 minutes.
Step 5: Spoon the quinoa mixture into the prepared bell peppers, filling them to the top. Place the stuffed peppers in a baking dish.

Step 6: Cover the baking dish with foil and bake in the preheated oven for 20 minutes. Remove the foil, sprinkle the tops with shredded cheddar cheese, and bake for an additional 5-10 minutes, or until the cheese is melted and bubbly.

Step 7: Remove from the oven and let cool slightly. Garnish with chopped fresh cilantro if desired. Serve warm.

Nutritional Values

Cal: 350

Carbs: 50 g

Sugar: 8 g

Protein: 15 g

Fat: 10 g

5.18 Roasted chicken with root vegetables

Prep time: 15 min
Cook time: 45 min
Serves: 2

Ingredients
- 1 small (about 1.5 lbs) whole chicken
- 1 tablespoon olive oil
- 1 teaspoon dried thyme
- 1 teaspoon dried rosemary
- 1 teaspoon garlic powder
- 1/2 teaspoon salt
- 1/2 teaspoon black pepper
- 2 medium carrots, peeled and cut into chunks
- 2 medium parsnips, peeled and cut into chunks
- 1 small sweet potato, peeled and cut into chunks
- 1 small red onion, cut into wedges
- 1 tablespoon fresh parsley, chopped (for garnish)

Method
Step 1: Preheat the oven to 400°F (200°C).
Step 2: In a small bowl, mix together the olive oil, dried thyme, dried rosemary, garlic powder, salt, and black pepper.
Step 3: Rub the seasoning mixture all over the chicken, making sure to coat it evenly.
Step 4: Place the chicken in the center of a roasting pan.
Step 5: Arrange the carrots, parsnips, sweet potato, and red onion around the chicken in the roasting pan.
Step 6: Roast in the preheated oven for 45 minutes, or until the chicken reaches an internal temperature of 165°F (74°C) and the vegetables are tender.
Step 7: Remove the pan from the oven and let the chicken rest for 10 minutes before carving.
Step 8: Garnish with chopped fresh parsley before serving.

Nutritional Values
Cal: 450
Carbs: 35 g
Sugar: 10 g
Protein: 40 g
Fat: 15 g

5.19 Mediterranean vegetable stew

Prep time: 15 min
Cook time: 30 min
Serves: 2

Ingredients
- 1 tbsp - Olive oil
- 1 - Medium onion, chopped
- 2 cloves - Garlic, minced
- 1 - Red bell pepper, chopped
- 1 - Zucchini, chopped
- 1 - Eggplant, chopped
- 1 can (14.5 oz) - Diced tomatoes, no salt added
- 1 cup - Low-sodium vegetable broth
- 1 tsp - Dried oregano
- 1 tsp - Dried basil
- 1/2 tsp - Ground cumin
- 1/4 tsp - Ground black pepper
- 1/4 tsp - Salt
- 2 cups - Fresh spinach
- 1 tbsp - Fresh parsley, chopped (for garnish)

Method
Step 1: Heat the olive oil in a large pot over medium heat. Add the chopped onion and minced garlic, and sauté until the onion becomes translucent, about 5 minutes.
Step 2: Add the chopped red bell pepper, zucchini, and eggplant to the pot. Cook for another 5 minutes, stirring occasionally.
Step 3: Pour in the diced tomatoes and vegetable broth. Stir in the dried oregano, dried basil, ground cumin, ground black pepper, and salt.
Step 4: Bring the mixture to a boil, then reduce the heat to low. Cover the pot and let it simmer for 20 minutes, or until the vegetables are tender.
Step 5: Stir in the fresh spinach and cook for an additional 2-3 minutes, until the spinach is wilted.
Step 6: Serve the stew hot, garnished with fresh parsley.

Nutritional Values
Cal: 220
Carbs: 30 g
Sugar: 12 g
Protein: 5 g
Fat: 9 g

6. 30-day diabetic meal plan

Week 1:

Monday:

- Breakfast: Almond and blueberry smoothie

- Lunch: Turkey and spinach stuffed peppers

- Dinner: Grilled salmon with dill yogurt sauce

- Snacks: Low-carb yogurt parfait

- Desserts: Chia seed pudding with berries

Tuesday:

- Breakfast: Spinach and feta omelette

- Lunch: Quinoa and black bean salad

- Dinner: Baked salmon with dill yogurt sauce

- Snacks: Protein-rich breakfast bars

- Desserts: Nutty banana bread

Wednesday:

- Breakfast: Cinnamon apple oatmeal

- Lunch: Mediterranean chickpea wrap

- Dinner: Butternut squash and chickpea curry

- Snacks: Cottage cheese and peach bowl

- Desserts: Ricotta and pear toast

Thursday:

- Breakfast: Avocado toast with poached egg

- Lunch: Grilled chicken caesar salad

- Dinner: Eggplant and mozzarella bake

- Snacks: Green detox smoothie

- Desserts: Chia seed pudding with berries

Friday:
- Breakfast: Low-carb yogurt parfait
- Lunch: Vegetable stir-fry with tofu
- Dinner: Shrimp and asparagus stir-fry
- Snacks: Sautéed mushrooms and tomatoes on toast
- Desserts: Nutty banana bread

Saturday:
- Breakfast: Turkey and spinach breakfast burrito
- Lunch: Zucchini noodle caprese
- Dinner: Balsamic glazed salmon
- Snacks: Cottage cheese and peach bowl
- Desserts: Chia seed pudding with berries

Sunday:
- Breakfast: Buckwheat pancakes
- Lunch: Lentil soup with spinach
- Dinner: Roasted chicken with root vegetables
- Snacks: Protein-rich breakfast bars
- Desserts: Ricotta and pear toast

Week 2:

Monday:
- Breakfast: Veggie-packed frittata
- Lunch: Avocado chicken salad
- Dinner: Mediterranean vegetable stew
- Snacks: Low-carb yogurt parfait
- Desserts: Nutty banana bread

Tuesday:
- Breakfast: Tofu scramble with kale
- Lunch: Cucumber and hummus sandwiches
- Dinner: Pork tenderloin with apple cider glaze

- Snacks: Green detox smoothie
- Desserts: Chia seed pudding with berries

Wednesday:
- Breakfast: Quinoa breakfast bowl
- Lunch: Lentil soup with kale
- Dinner: Stuffed acorn squash
- Snacks: Sautéed mushrooms and tomatoes on toast
- Desserts: Nutty banana bread

Thursday:
- Breakfast: Smoked salmon and cream cheese bagel
- Lunch: Shrimp and avocado taco salad
- Dinner: Vegetarian chili
- Snacks: Protein-rich breakfast bars
- Desserts: Ricotta and pear toast

Friday:
- Breakfast: Nutty banana bread
- Lunch: Broccoli and cheddar soup
- Dinner: Eggplant parmesan
- Snacks: Cottage cheese and peach bowl
- Desserts: Chia seed pudding with berries

Saturday:
- Breakfast: Sautéed mushrooms and tomatoes on toast
- Lunch: Asian beef salad
- Dinner: Baked tilapia with lemon and herbs
- Snacks: Green detox smoothie
- Desserts: Nutty banana bread

Sunday:
- Breakfast: Protein-rich breakfast bars
- Lunch: Quinoa and black bean stuffed peppers

- Dinner: Chicken and vegetable stir-fry
- Snacks: Low-carb yogurt parfait
- Desserts: Ricotta and pear toast

Week 3:

Monday:
- Breakfast: Scrambled eggs with spinach and tomatoes
- Lunch: Grilled chicken and avocado salad
- Dinner: Roasted salmon with steamed broccoli
- Snacks: Almond butter with celery sticks
- Desserts: Chia seed pudding with mixed berries

Tuesday:
- Breakfast: Greek yogurt with flaxseeds and berries
- Lunch: Quinoa tabbouleh with grilled shrimp
- Dinner: Zucchini noodles with marinara and turkey meatballs
- Snacks: Cottage cheese and cucumber slices
- Desserts: Nutty banana bread

Wednesday:
- Breakfast: Chia seed pudding with almonds and coconut flakes
- Lunch: Lentil and vegetable soup
- Dinner: Grilled chicken with roasted brussels sprouts
- Snacks: Green detox smoothie
- Desserts: Ricotta and pear toast

Thursday:
- Breakfast: Buckwheat pancakes with fresh berries
- Lunch: Tuna salad lettuce wraps
- Dinner: Stuffed bell peppers with quinoa and black beans
- Snacks: Almond and blueberry smoothie
- Desserts: Chia seed pudding with berries

Friday:

- Breakfast: Veggie-packed omelette
- Lunch: Shrimp and avocado salad
- Dinner: Grilled turkey burgers with roasted sweet potatoes
- Snacks: Cottage cheese and peach bowl
- Desserts: Nutty banana bread

Saturday:

- Breakfast: Tofu scramble with mushrooms
- Lunch: Broccoli and cheddar frittata
- Dinner: Baked tilapia with asparagus
- Snacks: Protein-rich breakfast bars
- Desserts: Chia seed pudding with berries

Sunday:

- Breakfast: Almond butter and banana toast
- Lunch: Mediterranean chickpea and kale salad
- Dinner: Grilled chicken with sautéed spinach
- Snacks: Green detox smoothie
- Desserts: Ricotta and pear toast

Week 4:

Monday:

- Breakfast: Greek yogurt with chia seeds and walnuts
- Lunch: Turkey and spinach salad with balsamic vinaigrette
- Dinner: Stir-fried shrimp with snap peas and garlic
- Snacks: Sautéed mushrooms and tomatoes on toast
- Desserts: Chia seed pudding with berries

Tuesday:

- Breakfast: Avocado toast with poached eggs
- Lunch: Lentil and quinoa salad with feta

- Dinner: Grilled salmon with roasted cauliflower
- Snacks: Cottage cheese and peach bowl
- Desserts: Nutty banana bread

Wednesday:
- Breakfast: Egg and vegetable frittata
- Lunch: Grilled chicken and kale Caesar salad
- Dinner: Zucchini and chickpea curry
- Snacks: Low-carb yogurt parfait
- Desserts: Ricotta and pear toast

Thursday:
- Breakfast: Quinoa breakfast bowl with almonds and cinnamon
- Lunch: Shrimp and avocado lettuce wraps
- Dinner: Turkey meatloaf with mashed cauliflower
- Snacks: Green detox smoothie
- Desserts: Chia seed pudding with berries

Friday:
- Breakfast: Low-carb yogurt parfait
- Lunch: Broccoli and cheddar quiche
- Dinner: Baked chicken with roasted root vegetables
- Snacks: Protein-rich breakfast bars
- Desserts: Nutty banana bread

Saturday:
- Breakfast: Buckwheat pancakes with almond butter
- Lunch: Asian chicken and cucumber salad
- Dinner: Grilled tilapia with zucchini noodles
- Snacks: Cottage cheese and peach bowl
- Desserts: Ricotta and pear toast

Sunday:
- Breakfast: Spinach and feta omelette
- Lunch: Mediterranean tuna salad

- Dinner: Grilled turkey burgers with mixed greens
- Snacks: Green detox smoothie
- Desserts: Chia seed pudding with berries

SCAN THE QR CODE

OR COPY AND TRY THE URL

https://qrco.de/bfTt6F

Printed in Dunstable, United Kingdom